Father To Son

Father To Son

◆

A Guide To Growing Up In A Difficult World

Reginald L. Bullock

Writers Club Press
New York Lincoln Shanghai

Father To Son
A Guide To Growing Up In A Difficult World

Writers Club Press
an imprint of iUniverse, Inc.

For information address:
iUniverse, Inc.
2021 Pine Lake Road, Suite 100
Lincoln, NE 68512
www.iuniverse.com

ISBN: 0-595-21673-0 (pbk)
ISBN: 0-595-74638-1 (cloth)

Printed in the United States of America

A Personal Note to my son

Reggie, today is December 21, 1993, and for several months I have been toying with the idea of writing you a Father to Son book in the event I become absent in your life. As you know, I was raised by my mother—your grandmother, Annie Marie (Bullock) Pompey. You also know I have never even met my father. Growing up without my father in my life has left a void that only he could fill. While it is very difficult to explain, it is easy to feel. Through this book, I will try to explain those feelings so that you may learn from my experiences without having to duplicate them all. Once I have completed this book—if that is possible; or rather terminated its continuance, perhaps I will also write one for your sister Chenae. Although she needs a father's wisdom as well, I am more intimately familiar with the course of growing up from boyhood to manhood than I am about womanhood. Reggie, this book is for you.

FATHER TO SON

By Reginald L. Bullock

Son, walk with me
that I may tell you all I have seen.
Wear my shoes,
that you may learn what I have learned.
Open your heart and mind,
that I may teach you the ways of the world.
Then stand on my shoulders,
that you may see further than I
and teach me all that you see.

Contents

PREFACE

I grew up without a father, I have studied other fathers, and most importantly, I am a father. In my opinion this qualifies me to speak and write on this subject. Although many people have told me that in spite of a lack of fatherly influences throughout my life, I turned out all right. I cannot help but wonder where I would be in life if I had my father present. Having grown up without him has left me with many unanswered questions, deep hurt, feelings of loneliness, and emptiness. Imagine asking your mother questions that your testosterone just conjured up, or trying to communicate certain issues to her and the look on her face tells you she has no understanding of what you are talking about. It gives you a feeling of abandonment when you grow up not ever having had the opportunity to speak to your father. It is being a bastard.

I have worked with young men from Cub Scouts, Weblos, Boy Scouts, Explorers, Civil Air Patrol, Reserves Officer Training Corps, Summer Camps, YMCA's, Recreation Centers, Gangs, Boys Clubs, Nights of Pythagoras, Churches, Mosques, Temples, Game Rooms, Sports Teams, Local Neighborhoods, and many other environments and organizations. It hurts to see many of them going through the same pains that I have had to go through. You can look into their faces and see the void. You feel their pain and hear their cries as they search for their identities. The fatherless son needs help. The fatherless son needs a father. He needs his father.

Due to the state of the world today, many young men are destined and doomed to grow up and develop into a man without a father. While the government and other institutions have been trying to deal with the problems of single parent families, the problems have continued to grow and solutions continue to be slow. Perhaps the old cliche,

"It takes one to know one," holds true in this instance. Generally the policy makers, thought provokers and instigators come from two parent families. Although they have tremendous insight with their statistical studies, they cannot feel what it is like. I have had to harbor feelings that will continue to plague me for the rest of my life, because I had no father in the house. These feelings run so deep, my mother is not even aware of some of them. In contemplating the chapters for this book, I cannot help but feel sorry and empathy for the many fatherless sons who were not as fortunate as I have been.

I do not want anyone to ever have to go through some of the experiences that I have gone through. So I am writing this book in hopes that an ounce of prevention is truly worth a pound of cure.

ACKNOWLEDGMENTS

To the single mothers and especially my mother, this book is by no means intended to demean the blood, sweat and tears you have shed in your efforts to raise a man. Without you mom, I would not be who and what I am today. Without you, I would not have learned the many things I did. And for those things, I owe a sincere debt of gratitude to you. It was you and you alone who picked up the dropped torch of fatherhood; and with all your strength, carried it as far as God has allowed you to carry it. So take your rightful seat of honor knowing that you have labored hard and the fruits of your labor have blossomed. It is just that my experiences have taught me: while a mother can raise a son, only a man can raise a man. I love you Mom.

To the stepfathers and other men who have adopted sons, I applaud you. You have taken on one of the most challenging responsibilities one could ever attempt. To the many men who have given their time, unconditionally, to fatherless sons, I commend you and thank you. You men are all forging a new generation of leaders and thinkers who will one day carry this great nation to higher heights. You should feel proud; for the best thing anyone could ever spend on a child is time.

To the fathers who have abandoned their sons to be raised as bastards, I blame you for many of our nation's problems. You will learn as you read this book how important you really are. You will learn how your absence has caused tremendous damage to the foundation of our families. Your absence has caused instability in our communities. Your absence has also incapacitated the most important resource of our country, your son. Indeed you are guilty; however, I challenge you to take charge of your responsibilities and redeem yourselves by raising your sons to be men.

I would also like to thank all of my family and friends for their encouragement and support over the years. It is always good to know you have someone to turn to when the going gets rough. In my lifetime I have had many, "going gets rough" days than I care to remember. In spite of myself and my ways, I always had a comfort net to fall into.

I would like to thank my daughter, Chenae, for reminding me of my fatherly duties, by making sure I gave her a good night hug and kiss in spite of how consumed I was in writing this book. You are my check and balance in many respects. Somehow you inherited most of my traits and genes. As I watch you grow, I am constantly reminded of how I was when I was younger. Sometimes, it's like looking back in time through a mirror. Watching you develop your mental abilities is going to be real interesting and at times maybe even scary. It is for those elements that you are very important in the writing of this book. Perhaps if I get the nerve, I will try to write one for you. In the mean—time, use this one as a repository of information. Not to mention a way to learn more about the male species.

As for my son, Reggie... If it were not for you, this book might not have even been a thought. After all, the title alone is 50% you. I must first and foremost thank God for bringing you into my life, and then I thank you for being who you are. From birth to now, you have always been an inspiration to me. Your calm power, sense of pride and com-passion for others is far more advanced than I could have ever been at your age. Although I am your father, sometimes I wonder where you get your intellectual insight. At age seven you had wisdom that I did not have even at the age of 12. It is because of these gifts you possess, that I will always be able to learn from you.

Finally, I would like to thank Esther, my wife, for tolerating my absence and presence through—out the course of writing this book. It seems like we have been together forever. Your patience and under-standing have made me who I am today. You helped me to go back to school and finish my degrees during some of the most difficult times in our lives. You tolerated my ideas and dreams even when it put the family on thin ice. Your fortitude, temperance, prudence and justice provided me the balance I needed to learn about myself and in spite of the mistakes I have made, you hung in there with me. You respected my privacy and identity by not trying to read the book, by not making contributions to it nor questioning me about the contents while it was being developed and written. I know how hard that was for you at times. Thanks for the respect.... For those reasons, if it were not for you, I would not be able to write this book. You were my support throughout. From Saudi Arabia, Dubai UAE, Philadelphia, New York, Tennessee, Virginia and Maryland this has been a long time coming and you helped to make it happen. Big ups and props to my Lady "B."

INTRODUCTION

<u>F</u>ather To Son, A Guide To Growing Up In A Difficult World is a no nonsense, non–fiction book which is targeted primarily to young men who are not being raised by their fathers, who need male guidance in their life, and/or, who just cannot find their way to the right path of manhood. Although it targets the young, many people from age 22 to 82 may find this book to be very helpful. The book addresses the current issues and problems that our youth have to deal with and why, from a father to son perspective. It also gives guidance and direction for those who might need it.

CHAPTERS 1, 2, 3, AND 4

The first four chapters: **<u>Guns, Gangs, Drugs and Law Violations</u>** explain why the problems are the way they are, as well as identify the causes of the problems. The chapters give helpful information and guidance on how to cope with and get through the difficult years of adolescence without falling into the trap of negativity. The chapters also cites examples and instances that I have seen and experienced as a youth and as an adult which will help the readers to associate their situations with what is being read.

CHAPTER 5

The chapter **<u>Homosexuality</u>** is a straight forward opinion on how many fathers view this subject. Too many young men are left to figure out what this group is all about and what position they should take regarding homosexuals. Whether a person is straight or gay, they will have to deal with this issue as a person. This chapter helps to give the reader a foundation from which to start.

CHAPTER 6

<u>Communication</u> has always been the number one problem behind most of our youths' problems. Being able to communicate with every human being you come in contact with takes a lot of work. Most people are not familiar with the basic parts of speech, let alone the basic elements of communication. This chapter tries by utilizing various languages and slang's, to explain the importance of learning how to communicate in various languages, dialects, cultural slang's and ethnicities. It is a unique chapter full of surprises and interesting words to help captivate the reader's interest in learning the art of communication.

CHAPTER 7

No matter who you are, you will always have problems and struggles to face. Consequently, the chapter **<u>Problems and Struggles</u>** is designed to remind the reader that history is filled with problems and struggles. The chapter explains why struggles are necessary and how to approach them. Using several quotes and phrases from people like Frederick Douglas, this chapter shows that the relationship between the past and the present is very similar. This helps the reader to understand that he can use the information from the past to chart his future.

CHAPTER 8

The chapter on **<u>Friendship</u>** shows through examples how relationships grow and die. For the reader who has a hard time understanding what friendship is all about and how to know when they have found a true friend, this chapter is ideal. From having friends of the same sex, to finding a spouse, this chapter gives the reader insight by example of how friendships are formed.

CHAPTER 9

The controversial subject **<u>Religion</u>** is extensively examined while trying not to sound too opinionated. Using facts, quotes and references, the book gives the reader a solid base of information to help determine the who, what, where, why, when, which and how. Islam and Christianity are both used as references and cross references to give the reader more than one perspective on religion. There is also a research section showing the translation and transliteration of the word Christ and its many derivatives. This shows the reader that all he reads in the holy book is not necessarily what was meant when it was written. The primary objective of the Religion chapter is to help the reader to select an appropriate religion with an objective frame of mind. It is also designed to help prevent the reader from becoming a victim of cults.

CHAPTER 10

Single parent mothers make up a large percentage of parents raising their young children. In explaining the theory that a mother can raise a boy, a mother can raise a child, but a mother cannot raise a man; the chapter **Mothers** is designed for the mother and the youth. It commends the mother for the job she has done, however, it explains that because a mother cannot raise a man, this is the stage where most of the problems occur. This chapter also ridicules the fathers who are not fulfilling their responsibilities. This is not only a very powerful chapter, it will be an emotional chapter for many of the readers.

CHAPTERS 11 AND 12

The two chapters **Health / Fitness** and **Hygiene** are very critical chapters. Most young men are not taught how to take care of themselves the way they should. While young ladies are trained at very young ages, young men are neglected. Most mothers cannot show a young man the proper way to wash his penis, which is the primary reason for all the young men constantly scratching. From head to toe the book explains in explicit detail how to take care of your body, groom yourself and several preventive measures for staying healthy. The chapter also covers sports, exercise, and even becoming a professional athlete. It's a must for all young men to read who have never had a good father to son talk on the subjects of health, fitness and hygiene.

CHAPTER 13

If it were not for sex, none of us would be here, yet we do not want young people to have sex. Why? The chapter <u>**Sex**</u> goes along with abstinence; however, it explains why at a level that young people can understand. It is obvious from the statistics and also because of our natural instincts that young people are going to have sex. This chapter cannot and will not stop everyone from doing it; however, it can give a deeper understanding of the ramifications and the responsibilities that are associated with having sex. It also explains the difference between having sex and making love through analogies that are more beautiful than passionate.

CHAPTER 14

Most successful people approach their craft as if it were a game. They learn the rules, master the game and win. The chapter, <u>**The Game**</u>, shows the reader how to interpret life and its many intricacies by restructuring the way it is viewed into the form of a game. Using the Constitution of the United States, the book dissects it's contents for the reader and interprets it from a Struggling Afro–American male's frame of reference to show that the rules can be interpreted in many different ways. With that example, the book goes on to explain how that same technique can be applied to school, employment, etc. It is a hard hitting chapter that uncovers some well masked truth about our U.S. Government.

CHAPTER 15

The chapter <u>**Tenets**</u> is designed to help the reader find balance in their lives. Many of today's youths have strayed from living up to the honorable tenets like integrity, courtesy, reverent, ethical and others that make us proud to be associated with outstanding people who possess these qualities. This chapter tries to bring that back into our youth. By utilizing the Boy Scout as an example and explaining the benefits of being a scout as well as explaining the definition of several tenets, the book gives strong feelings towards someone with such a character.

CHAPTER 16

Education, or the lack of, is one of our nations largest problems, yet results are not happening. This chapter blames our government for their incompetence, lack of vision and mishandling of the brains of our young U.S. citizens. It explains how the reader has to take responsibility for his own education because depending on the government or anyone for that matter will only result in his being mis–educated. This chapter also explains education from a common person's perspective rather than an aristocrat. This chapter's aim is to give the reader a sense of educational direction.

CHAPTER 17

Ethnic Origin is a very powerful chapter dealing with identity and the problems of race. Using the atrocities of history as a premise, this chapter shows that it's alright to know your roots; it's alright to be upset at what occurred; however, we have to build from the past to be able to over come in the future. It explains that the people of the past are not the people of the present. It also explains that no matter what color or ethnic origin you are, you need to be proud of your heritage and its contributions to the world. This chapter is full of self esteem building material.

CHAPTER 18

Life and Death is not as morbid as it is realistic. Too many people take life for granted and so many people are afraid of death. Using examples, this chapter gives life and death the respect it deserves. It also tries to show the significance of both, and how the reader fits into the scheme of things.

CHAPTER 19

<u>Words To Live By</u> is a collection of quotes and phrases that many fathers might like to pass on to their sons for them to live by. Some are famous sayings and some are original.

CHAPTER 20

<u>For Your Information</u> is a chapter of selected short writings to help inspire the reader to not only be himself, but to be the best at what he does. It's the kind of writing that people would like to copy and put up on the wall.

The topics, views and statements expressed in this book are personal opinions, views and statements. I welcome criticisms, analyses and reviews which may substantiate or disprove what I have written. It is not intended to be a textbook nor a lesson plan, but merely a guide for my son in the event I am no longer in his life. I began this book, "Father to Son," specifically for my son as a repository of information. I feel all sons should be invested with knowledge by their fathers so that they do not have to start from the beginning, making the same mistakes their fathers made. Although this book was meant to be privileged reading for my son, as I began getting deeper into the writing stages, I realized that such a book might be appreciated by more than just my son. After being encouraged by many people to publish it, I decided perhaps I should. Consequently, I have tried to write this book in such a manner that all who read it will be encouraged to reflect on their own life and experiences. Through this book I will often use "You" and "Son"; referencing my son Reggie. Feel free to substitute those words with any words or names you choose.

1

Guns

Son, on this day I am writing this sentence, you are now four years old and happy. You take one day at a time and seem to live as if the world is a playground. When I was four, I lived in the projects—the Richard Allen Projects in North Philly. My mother made sure I knew my address in case of an emergency. I still remember it to this day, it was 703 A Jessup Place, off of Brown street. Our unit was on the first floor, which allowed us to get robbed every now and then, and my mother could do nothing about it. Although my mother seldom allowed us to see her crying or her feelings hurt, in reflecting on the past, I am sure she cried often. At least once a week, the gang, *Wallace Street,* and the one whose turf I lived on, *1–2–P (Twelfth and Poplar),* would fight over something or another. Sometimes I could hear the bullets bouncing off of the trash dumpster. My mother would come and get us when that happened. One time (I think 1967) I got a toy machine gun for Christmas called a Defender Dan that shot real plastic bullets. I must have been either naive or crazy, but I mounted it on its tripod stand, put my helmet on along with a camouflage jump suit that

I also received for Christmas, loaded the belt of plastic ammo, and began shooting in the direction of the oncoming real bullets. Needless to say, my mother snatched me up and brought me into the house.

Son, never play in the midst of oncoming bullets. In retrospect, I could have been killed on several occasions right in front of my own home. I guess it was my destiny to grow up and have children of my own.

All guns have many purposes, but the number one purpose that seems to out weigh them all is that guns are designed to kill. The bottom line is, if you shoot and hit something alive with a gun, there is a good chance it will not be alive for long. Although I have never shot anyone with a gun, I have and do carry a gun from time to time for protection. I purchased my first gun (Smith & Wesson 44 Magnum) in 1985 while residing in Hampton Virginia due to a burglary. Someone broke into our house and stole several expensive items, as well as all of our jewelry. That same day, I purchased my gun and a home security system, just in case they returned for what they did not get. The next night they did return. Fortunately for them, the alarm system got them, instead of me.

As a child in the Projects, I could do nothing but feel bad for my mother because there was no man in the house to protect us. As an adult, I was going to defend my family and property against any intruder. Son, you have the right, as a man, to protect yourself and family against any aggression. Whether you are four years old or seventy–four, I want you to always carry a sense of honor and dignity, knowing that you are responsible for your family. As a father, I charge you with that responsibility.

Years later at the age of 11, I became a Boy Scout and learned how to handle and shoot a gun and rifle safely. We learned all the parts of the gun, and most importantly, we learned respect for the gun. Target shooting became fun and challenging as a sport. In May of 1982 I joined the Air Force and learned not only how to sight in and shoot an M–16 rifle, but how to take it apart, clean it, and put it back together.

This added a new dimension to my knowledge and respect for the gun. A gun is a tool, and like any tool its intended use is in the hand of the user. If the user chooses to shoot paper targets, game food, or humans it is all in their hands and mind.

In 1983 I joined the Rod and Gun club at Sembach Air Base, Germany, where I learned about shot guns. I also learned how to shoot the games of skeet and trap. While I did fairly well shooting skeet, I was terrible at trap. My favorite gun to shoot with for skeet was the Remington 1100 automatic. Although shooting skeet was fun, for an Airmen First Class it was expensive, so I could not shoot consistently twice a week to become very proficient. I was only 21 at the time, so most of the older guys looked out for me. Some even gave me free ammo and clay pigeons because they knew I did not have much money. Later on in the book I will devote some time to the subject of racism; however, I would like to point out to you that I was the only black person in the club. Yes, the club had a lot of so–called Red Necks, but they treated me with respect, and looked out for me.

Around October 1987, my wife purchased me a 30–06 Remington 7600 pump rifle for hunting purposes. I was really proud of that gun. I cleaned it all the time just so I could hold it. Every once in a while I would take it to the Shinnecock Indian Reservation for target practice and sighting in the scope. My brother–in–law and father–in–law, the late *Ferdinand Lee*, would also go with me. We three would have so much fun trying to outdo each other by hitting difficult targets at various distances. Your Grandfather would beat us every time with the 44 Magnum. He was only about 140 pounds; but he would stand facing the target with his bad knees slightly bent, his eyes focused in deep concentration; then through the silence of the woods (Boom) he would hit the target, turn and give us a half smile as if to say, "Was there any doubt?" Father, Son, and son–in–law; we had many moments like that. Those are the memories that I will never forget, and those are the kinds of memories that I hope you have the chance to experience.

Three men, having fun with a gun. There was nothing criminal about that. It was almost as good as going bass fishing.

Another interesting incident happened January 16, 1991 while I was an Air Force Recruiter. That was the day President George Bush declared Desert Storm open on Iraq. Due to the intense climate of the Gulf situation, Air Force Recruiters were directed to wear civilian clothing so as not to attract unnecessary attention. Because of the imminent hostilities from local civilian groups, several recruiters carried guns for personal protection. The night of January 16, 1991, several Air Force Recruiters, including myself, were at the pistol range target practicing when we heard the declaration of Desert Storm on the Television.

After hearing the news, we all decided to go home. At that time, I lived on the Naval Base. When I got to the front gate, I noticed that security was beefing up drastically due to the nature of the new security threat. The security guards stopped me and asked what was in the case on my back seat. I told them, "a gun." At that moment, they panicked and got hysterical. They made me get out of the car for a body search. After finding nothing, they then began to search the car. After finding only the gun in a locked case in the back seat along with the targets and the ammo in the trunk, they ran the drug and bomb dogs through my car. Not being satisfied with their results, they decided to try and detain me for questioning. I told them my gun was registered with the state of Virginia, Pennsylvania, the Air Force and the Navy, and I had the receipts of purchase.

Being the prejudiced type of people they were, they just disregarded my credentials and decided to arrest my gun until they ran all the checks they could to try and find something. After three hours of harassment and wasted time at their station, they allowed me to go home. They told me that I could retrieve my gun the next day, provided all their checks were negative.

The following day I went to pick up my gun, along with giving their chief a formal complaint letter. He personally apologized for the harassment and unnecessary handling of my gun. He said that due to the youth of the security and the excitement of the moment, it was just my unlucky night. Life in the Military . . .

Son, as you grow older, you will hear of incidents where children are killed from playing with a loaded gun found laying around the house. The quick answer, as a solution is to get rid of the gun. Many people will be very strong minded in saying that if the gun had not been in the house, the child would still be alive today. However, those same people are not equally quick to say get rid of every weapon in the house. All knives are weapons, matches are weapons, hazardous and flammable liquids are weapons, power and non–powered tools are also weapons. There are many weapons in the house that could kill or injure someone; so blaming it on the gun is not the answer. The answer lies somewhere between curiosity, education and miseducation.

Most children are not educated on guns. As with myths about the snake, Americans are brain washed into believing so many bad things about the gun, that it has caused many Americans to have a phobia toward guns. If children are taught the purposes, attributes, and benefits of the gun, in the same way that tools, electricity, the steam engine, and other items that were so beneficial to the early settlers are taught, then they would begin to understand that it is not just for gaining respect as seen on television. If children had the opportunity to shoot a gun in a controlled environment and learn how devastating it can be, then they would develop a respect for its power, similar to the way a child learns about hot water. It is all in how we are educated. Garbage in, garbage out.

When a child understands the devastation of a gun and what really happens after the bullet hits its target, they will not play with it as a toy; rather, they will treat it with respect. The problem that I have observed over the years is that many children, due to television and their parents purchasing them toy guns, cannot distinguish the difference until it is too late. As my son, I do not allow you to play with toy guns, nor do I allow your friends to bring them into my house. I am also strict about you allowing your friends to point guns at you—water guns, cap guns or just noise makers. I educate: never point a gun at anything unless you intend to kill it. This way if you are ever in a situation where your friend's parents are not as smart about toys as they should be, and your friend points a real gun at you in fun, you will quickly correct him and educate him in the absence of his parents.

While growing up, my friends and I started with noise maker guns. After a few years we needed more realism and stimulus so we graduated to water guns. When the water guns were no longer satisfying, our thrill seeking addiction to becoming like the heroes on television became so strong we escalated to BB guns. With BB guns, we were in the big time. We can hit targets and do damage. One of my friends used to sit at his bed room window and shoot girls on the butt passing by. He would brag about it every time he hit someone. As we got into the high school years, the BB gun became boring. If someone really wanted respect, a BB gun was not good enough. Blank guns became the new crave because they looked identical to a .22 pistol and could scare a person green. Some of my innovative friends drilled the barrel and put a real bullet in it . . . Yes it worked, but it was dangerous to the shooter as well as the target.

After the thrill of the toys wore off, the adrenaline to have *more* translated into the purchase of real guns. The rest is yesterday's, today's and tomorrow's news. This is the mis–education process of how many of our young gangsters, drug dealers and wannabes, came to be. It all started at home. After ten to fifteen years of brain washing a youngster with a gun in his hand, how can anyone put all the blame on him. Yes he did the crime, and yes it is his fault. My question, however, is, who do you think is at fault for him having the gun in his hand in the first place? That is the ten million dollar question and therein lies your ten billion dollar answer.

I recall an incident in the Air Force while stationed in Germany, when a young boy about eight years of age was playing with his water gun which looked real. He saw one of the security police officers coming near him and decided to have some fun. As the officer came close, the young boy yelled, "Put your hands in the air!" Catching the police officer off guard, the officer's instinctive reflexes took over. The officer drew his gun, pointed it at the young boy and shouted, "Drop your weapon or I will be forced to shoot you!" The young boy hysterically dropped his weapon in fright and began crying out of fear of being killed.

The little boy went into mental shock and required therapy to help him to resolve his fears. The officer was given a reprimand for drawing his weapon on the young boy—I do not recall if he was reduced in rank. All this from a toy gun incident. My question is; suppose the gun had been real—or worse yet, suppose the officer had shot the young boy? The bottom line is that because of a toy gun, they both experienced an unnecessary lasting impression on their lives more clinically called a significant emotional event.

Guns are made to be sold, not to sit on the shelf. The water gun, the cap gun, the blank gun, the BB gun, the noise maker, the cartoons, the television shows, the media and the so–called system—all contribute to the problem, but where can the solution be found? The answer lies all around us and right in front of us. The Father.

Every time I hear of a child being accidentally shot, by a loaded gun while playing, I feel bad inside. I feel bad because I know of someone personally who was also shot and killed by accident when I was a child. I feel for the parents because I too have children and I could only imagine the pain they must be going through from the loss of their child. While accidents do happen, we can decrease the amount through education.

You need to develop respect for the gun, not with the gun. You should learn how to shoot and become very accurate with your shots. Even when hunting, shooting a gun is very dangerous. It is especially dangerous when the shooter misses his target. A stray bullet has to stop somewhere. I do not want you to end up dead because of a gun. In today's society, young men are killing one another with all sorts of guns, but they are also killing many innocent people with their stray bullets.

The number one reason for the killing is not drugs, it is not the school system, it is not the television, and it is not the easy accessibility of the guns. All those variables have always been around. The real reason young men are killing each other is because they do not have a father in their lives. The real teacher is absent. The real instructor is missing after the action. The real professor of life's education is not there to teach them the thousands of lessons that develop young boys into productive men. Those are some of the real reasons our problems with guns are out of control.

Presently there are many politicians, lobbyists, organizations, parents and others trying to pass some sort of law on gun control. Some are even trying to go against the Constitution of the United States. Although I do agree that we must institute some sort of gun control on the automatic weapons, I disagree with changing the constitution.

Just because the citizens are not following the Constitution does not mean you can change it. It means you should enforce it. When we had slavery, the only thing we did with the Constitution was give more rights to citizens of the United States, not take away their rights. The killings, the gangs, the violence is all violation of our Constitutional Rights as citizens/taxpayers. For every violation committed, we are paying the United States Government cash money to secure the blessings of liberty to ourselves and our posterity. This means it is their job to not only prevent these violations from happening, but to stop them.

Rather than accept the blame and point the finger at themselves, politicians are running away from their responsibilities by pointing the blame at the ones with the guns. Personally I view the politicians and the rest of the governmental staff as my employees. I pay them to do a job. If they are not able to do the job, if they fail at the task given to them, or if they prove to be incompetent, then they should all be dismissed from their positions.

The United States Constitutional Amendments, Bill of Rights, Article II, The Right to Keep and Bear Arms, states: A well–regulated militia being necessary to the security of a free State, the right of the people to keep and bear arms **shall not** be infringed.

You do not need a first class over paid scholarly lawyer to interpret that basic right as a citizen. It was written to be self explanatory, not in code to be interpreted. The last four words <u>shall not be infringed</u> are also self explanatory. If this statement only meant a militia, then the entire judicial system is at fault for allowing guns to be in the hands of the public for this long since the amendment's first printing. I would also consider all the presidents who nominated the judges to the Supreme Court and all the politicians who confirmed the judges, all incompetent. If this were the case, then our entire United States Government is also incompetent. Since the United States is not incompetent, plain English should not be interpreted. It should stand as is.

Son, if I were to see or hear of you behaving in a manner which is contradictory to the path of righteousness, I would instantly alter your course and put you back on track. This is what our government is supposed to be doing for the people. I would overrule and override your decisions and help you to understand the why and how of life in a way only a father could do. A father is the foundation for his son, and a pillar in the family. Without the father as a foundation, it is difficult to build a man. Never forget that.

- Son, you learn right from wrong every day of your life.

- Whether a father is present or absent, it is incumbent upon you to always think before you speak or act so that you may make the right decision.

- Do not become a statistic because as you are learning, the constitution might not help you.

- Do not become blinded to the true meanings of life, liberty and the pursuit of happiness.

- Respect the gun, never be afraid of the gun; however, always remember, a gun is at it's most lethal state when it is in the hands of men and women.

- Never give up your rights as a United States citizen, your forefathers have already died for it.

2

Gangs

Son, just as I have some experience with guns, I also have experience
with gangs. In growing up in the inner city, I have seen and done more
than I could ever recall. One of the things I do remember is my
involvement in gangs. My first experience was in the Richard Allen
Projects with the two gangs Wallace Street and 1–2–P (12th & Poplar). Those two gangs fought over turf and women. There was a divid-
ing line which was actually a vacant lot around 12th and Brown street.
If either gang crossed it, that was grounds for a fight. The Wallace
street gang was Hispanic and the 1–2–P gang was black. I used to

admire the guys from the gang because they could fight and they had respect from their peers. I felt that they were "Cool."

Somewhere around November 1968 we migrated to another part of Philadelphia called Germantown. By 1970 at the age of eight I could not defend myself in a fight because I did not know how to fight. Although I wanted to learn, there was no one in my life to teach me. I had no father, so I had to solve my problems on my own, which generally resulted in me losing many fights. Most of the time after the fight, I would go somewhere and cry in private.

I would start off crying about the fight I lost. Then I would cry because I was all alone with my problems. I had no father to talk to and my mother did not understand. Once in a while I would talk to my younger brother who always seemed to understand and say the right thing. Although he is dead now, which I will elaborate on in another chapter, he was one of the smartest people I have ever known. Occasionally if he was around, he would jump into the fight and we would double team the person or lose together. I could always count on my brother and he could always count on me.

Losing a fight had many side affects. The girls would laugh at you in school and in the neighborhood, making it difficult for you to go anywhere in peace. You had no respect from anyone because you could not fight; you were a loser. Sometimes during a fight, if the person was winning easily, he would turn it into a game and give the crowd of onlookers a show. This would cause a great deal of embarrassment to me, which consequently decreased my self esteem. Life in those days where rough.

I remember one incident around 1971. We used to go to a recreation center, called the Morris Estate, after school until my mother picked us up on her way home from work. One day after my brother and I had finished track practice at the recreation center, someone started calling me names. Because I could not fight, I walked away. The guy followed and pushed on me while the on lookers kept growing. By the time a sizable crowd had evolved, he hit me. Just as he began to hit me again, I saw my mother and a sigh of relief came over me. Mom was here to save the day.

I screamed as loud as I could, "MOM!" She looked at me and said, if I did not hurry up and get into the car she was going to leave me. All I can remember is that she turned her back and walked away with my brother to the car. I got beat up by several people before the recreation director came out and saved me. Perhaps if I had a father, things would have turned out differently. Maybe that is why martial arts training is a daily aspect of my life now. While having a black belt does not mean you can fight, having the knowledge and training of a black belt, along with a determination of never allowing a person to harm you or your family does give you more confidence. On that premise, I encourage everyone to learn some form of martial arts. The confidence alone will help you.

After that fight, I met a guy who treated me like his little brother. I guess he was about 19 or 20. He and I became good friends and when he was around, no one tried to challenge me. He had the respect of everyone who came in contact with him. I later found out that he was the leader of a gang called *"Clang."* I remember one afternoon there where reporters and television cameras around the recreation center. I saw my friend and asked what was going on. He told me that in order to keep good relations with the police, he was publicly handing over several hand guns and shot guns that his gang owned. I remember being proud to know him.

Although he did not tell me much about the internal workings of his gang, he did tell me that they used to fight other gangs by the name of *"Brick Yard, Nice Town, and Somerville"* (pronounced <u>Somvill</u> in slang). I recall hearing over the loud speaker while in class at John L. Kinsey elementary school, the Principal making an announcement that there was going to be a gang war in the school playground after school and for us to go directly home. We would hear that type of announcement at least twice a month.

Around age 12, or the beginning of the sixth grade, I stopped going to John L. Kinsey because I was transferred to a newly built school in my neighborhood called Ada H.H. Lewis middle school. Although the school was new, the neighborhood was old. This school sat right in the middle of *Somerville's* turf. Just across the school yard was the Martin Luther King high school. That is where the older members of the *Somerville* gang went to school. What's more, I lived two blocks from both of these schools, which meant geographically I lived in *Somerville*. I quickly remembered that my friend was the leader of the gang called *Clang* and did not like *Somerville*. I had to make a choice . . . Later the choice was made for me. I was sort of drafted into the gang *Somerville* based on where I lived. I recall one of my friends being drafted by a gun pointed to his forehead. So when the crew made it around to me, I quickly accepted their request. After that, I never ventured back to the old recreation center for fear of having to hurt, or be hurt by my old friends.

Somerville's rival gang was the *Haines Street* gang. Unfortunately the city did not care about mixing gangs because they had both gangs in the same school. After school, on many occasions, we would meet in the park across the street from the school and fight *Haines Street*. Sometimes people got stabbed, but most of the times it was just fist and feet, which only left bruises. On the rare occasions that someone pulled out a gun and fired it, everyone would scatter because no one knew whose side possessed the gun.

My gang, *Somerville,* even had a subsidiary, or several for that matter. There was an inner group called the *Shank Squad.* Although I did not know all of the members, I was familiar with their reputation. Their job was to stab and slice people. For a while I wanted to become a member, then reality set in. *Somerville* was a large and well–respected gang in Philadelphia. Because we were so large, several friends–including myself–decided to start our own gang because *Somerville* was more dangerous than we wanted to be. We were concerned about protecting our turf and each other, but we were also interested in other things like school, boy scouts, business, etc.

Thus was born a new gang called, "*The Family.*" We did not restrict it to just males, we had females also. Later we added the K–9 squad which consisted of dogs. One dog was named Major, another named King and the rest I cannot recall. We would practice our fighting skills at least three times a week with each other, just for the fun of it and for people like me to learn new skills. We trained in boxing, karate, judo, wrestling, and weapons. Although we did not go looking for trouble, if ever someone bothered one of us, we would establish ourselves. We never had any run ins with *Somerville* because we were all from the same neighborhood established for the same cause, and some of us were former members of *Somerville*. We would however, just to keep good relations, challenge Somerville in boxing, football, basketball and other light contact sports. Nothing serious that would end up in a severe fight or injury.

Speaking of injuries, I lost a very good friend to gang violence. He was from *Somerville*. We met while at John L. Kinsey elementary school. He used to keep the bigger guys from beating on me and taking my money. When we went to the YMCA for sponsored after school activities, he would make sure the bigger guys did not rough me up unnecessarily. I remember he and I were pulling hall duty one day. (That's keeping the other kids from loitering in the halls, and watching the exit doors so that gang members could not gain access.) We went up on the roof of the school by way of a back stage access ladder in the auditorium. It felt like we were on top of the world because we could see all over Philadelphia (or so it seemed at the time). We spotted an empty beer bottle and my friend thought it would be fun to throw it off of the roof. He tossed the bottle over the edge without looking to see if anyone was below. We waited for the usual crash of the bottle, but instead it made a different sound. We looked over the edge to see what he hit.

A young boy about age 10 was laying on the ground in a pool of blood. Apparently all the kids were lined up to go inside after recess. The bottle hit the kid right on the head. To make matters worse, it was the son of one of the nicest teachers in the school. We felt really bad for the boy, but also scared for our own selves. We quickly got off the roof and decided that we would forget we were ever up on the roof. We never got caught. He never told on me, and I never told on him. I guess that is what "down by law" means.

Years later, that same friend was murdered by the *North Philly* gang in West Philadelphia. There are many speculations as to why he was killed, but the how part was obvious. He was shot many times in the chest and thrown out of a moving car in front of a moving bus that rolled over top of him. Although gang members were killed from time to time, his death hit home hard. Not just to me, but to the whole neighborhood. He was one of the few genuinely nice guys. He was always a gentleman to the ladies. His language was not foul like one would expect from a gang member. He had morals and was a role model to me and others. He was my close friend; he used to protect me from the bigger guys, and now he is dead. It could have easily been me lying there and him thinking about me. Nevertheless, dying at age 15 is sad, no matter how it comes.

These experiences and more are all results of gang affiliation. The unfortunate problem is that there was little I could have done to change anything, other than never coming out of the house. Perhaps if I had a father around, the members would not have drafted me. Some of the guys who did have fathers living with them, carried a different attitude. I would hear some of the members say things like, "Yo, don't mess with such and such man, his dad don't play that shit."

One time while throwing snow balls at cars, a car doubled back without us knowing it. Apparently the driver of one of the cars we hit, doubled back, got out of the car and snuck up behind us. As he was running down the snowy hill from behind us, one of the guys spotted him and said, "Break!" We all responded to the signal in the usual fashion by getting out of dodge. After meeting up at the designated rendez-vous, we realized that one of us was missing. We went to his house and found out that the man had caught him, beat him up, and cracked several of his ribs. The thing that really sticks in my head was his father's anger. His father grabbed a double barrel shotgun and told us to show him where it occurred. He was on a mission to kill the man who hurt his son. Although my friend was hurt very badly, I was also hurt because I did not have a father who would come to my rescue if anything like that ever happened to me. Moments like that make you think about those sort of things.

There was one occasion when I was swooped (that means beat up by many people at the same time). A guy from the *Haines Street* gang who I had a run in with, at a Bible Camp no less, spotted me on his turf. I was selling door to door household products for a company called Kathy Distributors. He must have spotted me earlier and gathered his boyz before confronting me, because while standing on a corner with my sales partner, waiting for our pick up, a guy came up to us and inquired about our products in the bag. Being from the streets, my sixth sense told me something was wrong. Just as I started to put my hand in my pocket for my knife, the guy yelled across the street, "Is this the guy?" Then a voice (sounding like the guy from camp) answered, "Yeah, that's the guy!" When I turned to see where the other voice was coming from, I was sucker punched in the head so hard, he knocked me on the ground. I landed on my elbow and was unable to get to my knife because my arm was out of commission from the fall. The next thing I knew, about eight guys came running from across the street and began punching me and kicking me.

When I heard one of them say, "Let's kill him!" I started punching back and managed to get back on my feet. I heard someone else say, "Let's shoot him!" I then started running down the street as fast as I could. I turned one corner, then down a driveway, up another street and to a phone booth where I called my mother who came right away and picked me up. After being home for about one hour, my mother's boyfriend came by. I related to him what happened. He then checked to see that he had a fully loaded gun and told me to get into the car and show him where the incident took place.

We found the gang sitting on the porch of one of their houses. He told them that what they did to me was not fair and if they were real men, they would have fought me one on one. He then told them that I would fight any of them right now, one on one if they so desired. I wanted to regain my dignity by fighting the leader, but he would not come down. My mother's boyfriend issued them a warning to stay away from me. Many incidents occurred similar to that in the past when I wished I had a father to help me. At least this time I felt confident that they would not bother me again.

I am telling you this to let you know that I have been there. I have been in so many situations similar to that one, I could go on and on. I know the streets better than most people who know me could ever imagine. Gang banging is real. Dying is real. Only now it is not as physical as it was when I was a boy. When I was a teenager, if you could or could not fight, you knew your place. Now it is guns, guns, guns. Gone are the days when you call someone out for a "fair one" (hand to hand fighting) and a crowd of onlookers encircle you to cheer on their preferred choice. That is how boxers evolved. You do not get too many second chances with the gun.

Gangs are real, and they exist for real reasons. I cannot predict your future or determine it for you. I can only share with you some of my experiences so that you do not make the same mistakes I made. The need to belong is a very powerful weakness that most of us have. There is a theory called Maslow's Theory of Hierarchy which you need to familiarize yourself with. It will show you that gangs exist because they need to exist. There are all sorts of gangs. Some violent and some not. Being in the Boy Scouts is a form of gang membership. Being a member of a fraternity is a form of gang membership. Being a member of Congress or City Council is a form of gang membership. The Chamber of Commerce, the Klu Klux Klan and Majestic Eagles are also gangs. Some of these types of gangs and many more like them are no different from the gang I was involved in. In fact, several well established organizations and businesses even started out as young gangs.

No matter where you are or where you go, you will always be around various types of gang environments; therefore, you must choose your gangs carefully. You must decide which gangs you want to be a part of and which gangs you need to stay away from. Only you can make that choice. I can only guide you.

3

Drugs

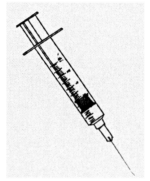

ALCOHOL

 Son there are some things about me, even if I told you, you would have a hard time believing it. Yes I have experimented with drugs, and no I am not going to list them. Let us look at why I did drugs. The first drug I experimented with is probably one of the most dangerous drugs on the market. It has killed more people than any other drugs I know of. It comes in thousands of varieties and has thousands of levels of potencies. It was the first drug I used and I am happy to say, I have kicked the habit. Alcohol... Alcohol is pure poison. I could tell you so many stories of myself in an inebriated state it would turn your stomach. I drank because my friends drank. I drank because it was the cool thing to do. I drank because all the cool guys on television drank. I drank because the commercials and adver-

tisements told me to. I drank because I thought it would help me erase my problems. I drank because I wanted to prove I was a man. I drank because my mother drank, (on occasions). I drank because I wanted to feel grown up. I drank because I did not know better. All the reasons I have given are just excuses.

I almost crashed my mother's car a couple of times. I almost crashed my car several times. I fell asleep at the wheel and had to pull off to the side of the road. Fortunately I have never crashed. I have blown lots of money because I was intoxicated/drunk. Contrary to popular belief, according to the National Safety Council, coffee is not successful at sobering up a drunk person, and in many cases it may actually increase the adverse effects of alcohol. Alcohol is a very dangerous drug and yet the government is probably the biggest dope pusher of them all. Did you know that one out of every thirteen adults over twenty years of age in the United States is an alcoholic? From them, the government literally makes millions of dollars and loses millions of dollars because of the sales and consumption of alcohol.

The taxes received from the sales of alcohol generate an enormous amount of revenue for the government. A good research project would be to trace where every penny received by the government in the name of alcohol went. It would also be interesting to learn how the decisions for allocations of that money is made. As a citizen, we are entitled to know where, how and why our tax dollar is spent, yet most of us do not even care. Try it one day.

Although it would be easy to say our government receives money in the name of alcohol, it should also be noted that our government also loses millions of dollars because of this drug. The accidents, deaths, hospital bills, court cases, prison terms, policemen man hours, abandoned children, battered spouses, public service announcements, paper work, paper, and red tape are all withdrawing cash money from our governmental funds. Those funds are our tax dollars which should be going to our educational and development programs. According to the National Institute of Alcohol Abuse and Alcoholism, liquor may be involved in as many as half the traffic fatalities that occur in the United States. Try contacting the Bureau of Alcohol, Tobacco and Firearms and see what statistical information they could send you for free. When contacting them remember, any gang with the word bureau in it uses red tape to hold everything together, so be patient and tenacious.

In any religion you have do's and don'ts. There are scriptures, commandments and sunna's to guide you along the righteous path in life, yet alcohol is even in the churches. You can be served wine for free in some churches. While I strongly believe in a Supreme Being, I disagree with hypocrites. There are many good Preachers, Ministers, Clergy, Priest, and Imams who would probably agree with me, but there are also those with the holy book in one hand and the bottle in the other. Be careful who you put your trust in.

I remember when I was about 14 years old, we would get several quarts of Old English 800. Talk about cheap. This stuff was the cheapest we could get, but it was potent. We would drink until we threw up sometimes, then we would drink some more. We played all sorts of games where the looser had to take a drink.

I remember one time, I got so inebriated I had to call my wife to come and pick me up. The worse part was that I was in uniform. Because I was a recruiter for the Air Force with an office located in downtown Philadelphia, it did not matter if I was off the clock. If I had been seen by the wrong people, I would have been in the news papers the next day. "Air Force Recruiter, Staff Sergeant Bullock was too drunk to walk while vomiting in the street." I would have brought discredit upon the Air Force, my country, my family, my friends, and myself. Thank goodness for close friends who did not let that happen. Looking back on my drinking days, I try to search for one thing positive about drinking. I cannot find anything positive about drinking that would not have been better if I had not drank.

There are many myths surrounding alcohol which many people believe in. One myth that has been perpetuated for a long time, is drinking to keep warm. Actually, drinking lowers rather than raises the body temperature. There is an illusion of heat because alcohol causes the capillaries to dilate and fill with blood. In very cold weather, drinking alcoholic beverages can lead to frostbite. Generally the person drinking is usually too drunk to realize his body's warning signs before hurting himself. If you can go through life without having to drink alcohol, you are better off than those that do. However if you cannot, please, please, please, drink responsibly, if there is such a thing.

CIGARETTES

Cigarettes is another type of drug that I used to do. Unlike the alcohol, I was addicted to cigarettes. I started smoking at age 12. We would sneak and do it whenever we could. After a few years I was hooked. There are several reasons why I started. Perhaps the most logical reason was because my mother smoked. I remember telling her to quit when I was about seven or eight. She said she would give me and my brother Bernard one quarter every time we caught her smoking. That did not last long. I recall while living in the projects, when we were about four or five, my mother would put us to bed, and if we were good, she would twirl the cigarettes around with the lights out. We would watch the red part glow and move about as if it were magic. What a treat...

Perhaps commercials, perhaps peer pressure, perhaps the glamour; whatever started me smoking it was not good. Cigarettes have also killed more people than the tobacco companies care to admit. Smokers suffer 65 percent more colds, 167 percent more nose and throat irritations, and have a 300 percent greater incidence of chronic coughs than nonsmokers. It is even possible to go blind from smoking too heavily. A condition known as amblyopia, in which a person's sight grows progressively dimmer is directly attributed to excessive use of cigarettes. The cure is usually quite simple: Stop Smoking. The amount of nicotine the average pack–a–day smoker inhales in a week –400 milligrams– would kill a person instantly if it were taken in all at once. My father–in–law died because of cigarettes. We watched him slowly fade away over several months in the hospital from cancer. Just before he died, he told my wife and I we were going to have a boy. He was right.

 Although quitting the habit of smoking was very difficult for me, the real test is to never pick another one up. I have seen many people try to quit and I have come to a hypothesis on quitting a bad habit. You can only quit if you have a strong enough reason to quit. I read lots of literature on the harmful and lasting effects smoking causes; but the two most important reasons I quit are still vividly in my mind to this day. One reason was because a friend who had stopped for over ten years told me that he can look at anyone and tell if they smoked because they start to develop skin blotches around the back of the neck. He said he could also tell approximately how long that person smoked or how much they smoked by how wide spread these blotches were. I began to see these blotches on people who smoked, but not on me yet. Perhaps there was hope after all.

The other reason, which was the one that made me throw away all ashtrays, lighters, cigarette cases, and any other cigarette paraphernalia I possessed was my son and daughter. My daughter walked up to me for a hug when she was about two years old while I had a lit cigarette in my hand. She came at me so fast, I did not have time to react. I burned her forehead and she started crying. Every day I had to look at my pretty little daughter knowing I had disfigured her unsacred skin. After several weeks of that incident haunting me, I quit. I was afraid of that incident happening again. Since then, I have witnessed careless acts of smokers, and every time I see such an act, it reminds me of how I once burned Chenae. She has since healed and there is no trace of the burn. If you were to search your mind, I am sure you could list many careless acts you may have seen or heard of. Burn stains in the ceiling of cars, the burn marks on bed lining, tables and floors, fires, death by accidental fires, etc.

Cigarettes also have a distinct smell that never seems to go away. Generally if you are a smoker, you do not notice it. To a non–smoker the smell is as present as a men's bathroom that has never been cleaned. It stinks. The smell gets into your clothing hanging in the closet, so no matter what you wear, people will know you are a smoker. It stains the ceiling and walls brown with a film that is difficult to remove. It gets into the air conditioning system of your house and car so that every time you turn on the air conditioner, the cigarette smell circulates and permeates your breathing air with a distinct odor.

When people who smoke talk to you, sometimes their breath can be so foul smelling like tar, you tend to keep a comfortable distance away from them so as not to smell it. As a matter of fact, a person who smokes one pack of cigarettes a day, inhales a half–cup of tar every year. Even if you shake a smoker's hand, it is present. The smoker has just transferred the smell to you with their hand shake. Don't smoke. Medically and aesthetically it is not good for you.

Chewing tobacco, dipping snuff, or putting any type of tobacco products in your system, for that matter, is hazardous to your health. You can get cancer of the gums from chewing that stuff. If the Surgeon General of the United States has issued a printed warning on the packages of all the products and you still insist on using it, you have a fundamental problem.

After I finally quit smoking, I began to feel better, although I had gained ten pounds. I began to smell things I had not smelled in a long time. My food tasted better and my stamina increased. I was finally a non–smoker. My life insurance policy premium decreased. I had more money in my pocket because cigarettes were $1.25 per pack and at ten packs a week, that was a considerable savings over a period of time. The list of benefits from quitting goes on and on. I felt like I was freed.

Son, if ever you feel the temptation to smoke or if ever you are pressured by your so called friends to smoke, think about how it effected your grandfather and me. Cancer can truly shorten your life span. There is nothing good about smoking. The average smoker, the smoker who inhales one and a half packs of cigarettes a day, smokes 10,950 cigarettes a year. A heavy smoker may smoke as many as 30,000 cigarettes a year. A nonstop chain smoker may smoke as many as 40,000 cigarettes a year. All the reasons anyone can give you to smoke are just lies. People smoke because they are addicted to the drug. It is not for nerves, not for weight loss and not to calm them down. It is all a crutch, because they are afraid of facing the reality that they are drug addicts. They are weak minded individuals caught in the web of destruction. In the 1950's the government helped to promote cigarette usage. Radio and television advertised cigarettes as being the in thing. It was hip to be a smoker. Now the government is spending lots of our money trying to clean up the mess it helped to create. Don't smoke! Smoking will kill you and others around you. Don't just say, "No." Mean, "No."

ILLEGAL DRUGS

As for marijuana, hash, crack, cocaine, ice, acid, black beauties, uppers, downers, and all the other exotic stuff on the market, it is unnecessary. Your body has natural chemicals, which if caused to shift off balance, could be detrimental to your health. I have known personal friends who died from drugs. Some physically dead and some brain dead. I have one friend who was a promising athlete. He even won the golden gloves as a boxer. Now he walks the streets like a dazed zombie existing like a vegetable. I feel sorry for him, but he did it to himself. Perhaps if he had a father around, handling fatherly responsibilities, he would have become that promising athlete. It is a shame.

Look at the life of Brother Malcolm X. He started off with his father present which implanted the desire to be a Lawyer in his mind. He wanted to be a great man. A righteous man. After he lost his father, the lack of fatherly guidance was reflected in his negative direction and new found ambitions of crime. While in prison, he gained a new father (Elijah Muhammad) who put him back on track. He studied the truth and began to teach his brothers. Every time he uncovered new truths he shared them with everyone. Each of us must make our own choices in life, but when the truth is revealed, we should at least listen.

Son, it is all poison. While the government is spending millions of dollars trying to define and deal with the problems, they are wasting good tax money—my money, your money. . . I am here to tell you to deal with the symptom. Educate yourself on drugs and its effects on the body. Go to the library and research the drugs on the streets. Learn their chemical make–up and harmful effects. Use the knowledge to teach yourself and your friends the truth. You are a descendent of Kings. That means you have responsibilities. If you do drugs, then all the younger people who look to you for guidance will also do drugs. If you sell drugs, then all the young people who look up to you for guidance will also sell drugs. Conversely, if you do well in school, and become successful on your own terms with your own talents, then likewise will the younger people who look to you for guidance. The cycle of negative or positive growth starts with you. Make the right choice.

SELLING DRUGS

As for selling and dealing drugs, it is a rough life. Many of my former classmates from school and neighborhood friends are selling drugs. A few of them are doing extremely well financially. They have nice clothes, expensive cars, a wad of money in their pocket, and babies. On the surface, it all looks good, but all that glitters is not necessarily gold. They have to watch their back 24 hours a day. Not only must they watch their back, they must look out for their families as well. By dealing drugs, they put their mothers, brothers, sisters and whom ever else is close to them in danger. People's mothers have been killed because their children were dealing or using drugs.

Speaking of death, generally a drug dealer's career is short lived. If they are not caught and jailed for a few years, generally they stand a pretty good chance of having a short life. Since competition is the number one factor in the decrease or increase of the profit margin, logic tells you if you take out your competition you will increase your profits. The laws of economics causes the dealer to kill or be killed.

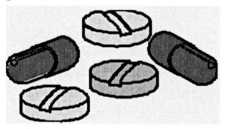 I could go on and on attacking the drug dealers, however, it is also necessary in their defense that I explain how they ended up as dealers. Reverting back to the father, many did not have a stable home. Although you will hear statistics point out many other factors, the bottom line is that by the time they become teenagers their mothers can not control them. Without parental control, teenagers are privileged to choose their own path. If you choose not to do your homework, if you choose not to study and achieve in school, if you choose to cut classes and hang out rather than hang in, if you choose not to listen to the experiences and wisdom of positive people, then your choices for employment are very slim. You lack the qualifications to get hired in the so called real world, so you seek employment in the under world.

Because your ability to read is not at the level it should be, filling out applications can be a scary, demeaning and intimidating experience. Because the system is extremely stereotypical, employers are afraid to hire you if you look like the image that frightens them, or the one that attacked them and stole from them once upon a time. On the flip side, one of my closest cousins went to school, received a bachelors degree, a Masters in Business Administration (MBA), and got a well paying stable job with all the perks as a Pharmaceutical Sales Representative (Drug Dealer) for one of the largest companies in the industry. After a few years he was so good another pharmaceutical company gave him a better offer to come work for them as their Mac Daddy over all the other sales representatives. Now he is making six figures plus. . . I told you the government was the largest drug dealer in the world.

What is the difference? Good question. Although I am not qualified professionally to answer that question, as a father I am compelled to give you a truthful reply based on my experience. The Government has the EPA (Environmental Protection Agency), FDA (Food and Drug Administration), and other organizations to attempt to control the harmful effects and side effects drugs can cause to the human body. They also have the FBI (Federal Bureau of Investigation), CIA (Central Intelligence Agency), DEA (Drug Enforcement Agency), and other organizations to monitor and control the legal exchange of these drugs. There are also millions of rules and regulations governing the sale, purchase and consumption of these drugs. This all spells control. There is a large control factor involved which is designed to keep us safe.

Now let us look at the street side of the house. The street does not have any organizations checking its harmful effects or side effects. If someone is distributing bad drugs, you can best believe that there will not be a recall or restitution made to the victims. Should a death occur from drug usage, I am sure the drugs will not be pulled from distribution.

There are organizations controlling the exchange of the drugs, but most of them are not legal. As for the rules of the game... It depends on what level you are at. The higher the level, the more rules you have to play by. The lower the level, the less rules you have to play by. The killing problem is generally at the lower levels because as dealers move up they do not adapt to the new rules. They continue to operate by the old rules—survival of the fittest. However, any killings at the higher levels are usually done after calculated thought, not arbitrary.

HISTORY

Drugs have been around and will always be around. It is said that some of our well known candy factories years ago used to coat their candies with drugs, causing kids to become addicted; thus constantly coming back for more. Sugar and Cocaine seem to have very similar effects.

Speaking of cocaine, it is said that Benjamin Franklin and others of that time, used cocaine quite regularly. As a matter of fact, both George Washington and Thomas Jefferson grew Cannabis sativa (marijuana) on their plantations. It is also said that the Indians never smoked until it was introduced by Europeans, and the peace pipe contained more than tobacco to ease the mind.

In 1865 opium was grown in the state of Virginia and a product was distilled from it that yielded 4 percent morphine. In 1867 it was grown in Tennessee; six years later it was cultivated in Kentucky. During these years opium, marijuana, and cocaine could be purchased legally over the counter from any druggist. Remember the world renowned and famous movie "The Wizard of Oz?" Think hard, what did the Wicked Witch use to put Dorothy and her companions to sleep? "Poppy, Poppy will put them to sleep", she said. What is poppy? Any of various plants having showy red, violet, orange, or white flowers, as the opium poppy. The flower of the poppy in art is the symbol of sleep or death.

I have told you all this information to give you a foundation of knowledge to use as you contemplate decisions concerning drugs. Whether it is legal or illegal, before having anything to do with drugs, it is incumbent upon you to think, think, think. Remember, tobacco and alcohol are both legal drugs, however, they are as harmful as the illegal drugs. Whether you are a pharmaceutical sales representative or a local drug dealer/trafficker, drugs are big business for big dollars which can cause big problems. History tells us that drugs have always been around, but the present tells us we have not learned from that history. We are still repeating the mistakes made in the past.

Drugs can do a lot of things. Some save lives and some take lives. Just as with the gun, the real power of drugs is not in the drug itself. It lies within us, how we choose to use it and administer it.

4

Law Violations

This chapter is not intended to explain the constitution or governmental legalities, it is intended to help keep you out of trouble through the use of preventive maintenance. Although I am not a Lawyer, I am familiar with some portions of the law, and through these familiarities, I wish to pass on to you some valuable information.

Law violations occur when you violate the law. The problem that seems to happen among many people, especially young people, are they usually do not know the effects that can occur from breaking the law. This is the part I want to convey to you. The effects on your life, liberty and pursuit of happiness can be dampened a great deal, depending on what you have on your record. Anything from a simple parking ticket, bad credit or drinking under age to murder goes on your record. Generally anything that goes on your record remains there permanently. I do not care what the officials tell you, if it went on your record it is probably still there. The dictionary defines record as: an account in written or permanent form serving as a memorial or evidence of a fact or event.

The reason you must be cognizant of your record, is to help you be very careful with any and everything you say and do. As an Air Force Recruiter in downtown Center City Philadelphia, I have seen or heard of almost every type of law violation a young person could have. From pool hopping to spitting on the curb, from protecting one's mother to defending a girlfriend's honor, no matter what the story was, the outcome was on record. One guy apprehended a young man who attacked and assaulted a women. Because he had to use force to apprehend the attacker, the attacker was able to press charges against the young man for assault. Although he did not serve time or pay any fines, the young man now has a record.

There is a legal term called *consent decree* that constantly came up during my investigation of applicants. I would be told by the applicants, lawyers, clerks and even Judges, that if the disposition was consent decree the violation no longer existed on record. Wrong answer. There is a record still existing somewhere. Sometimes the applicant told me he was acquitted, or his record was expunged. That still does not mean he did not do the violation. It means he was not found guilty. The only acceptable disposition to any violation is _DROPPED_ or _DISMISSED_.

The court system is so backed up, you would have to use a 50–ton laxative to clear it up. The system has become so impersonal, the priority now seems to be volume: Clear as many cases as possible per day. If you do not have a lawyer and sometimes even if you do, the system will railroad you through so fast, you will not even know what happened.

This is how people end up with a disposition they might not deserve. They never knew what hit them.

I had to disqualify so many people trying to get into the United States Air Force based on law violations. I became an expert on writing requests for waivers. The Air Force, as well as other governmental and professional organizations to include many of the fortune 500 companies, all require a background investigation in many cases before hiring anyone. For many of my applicants, a $15.00 parking ticket prevented them from entering the Air Force. Even truancy from school becomes part of their record as a law violation, which also prevented people from getting into the Air Force.

I recall an incident that almost tarnished my record, which happens daily to many people. One day (spring 1979) I was at a bus stop in the rain waiting for the bus to go to work. A police car pulled up next to me with two officers inside who told me to get into the car. I said, "what for?" They said, "Nigger, get your ass in the car!" So I got into the car. They drove me a couple of blocks to a lady's house and told me to get out of the car and walk slowly to her door until they told me to stop. As I walked to the door, the lady looked me up and down slowly and replied that I did not look like the guy who stole her television set. The police said, "Are you sure, look again." She looked at me again and said she was sure. That was a sign of relief. I got back into the car and the police officers dropped me off at a different bus stop in the Haines Street Gang territory. I asked them to take me back to the bus stop where they first picked me up, and they said, "You know your way around," and left me there.

That incident could have caused me to have an infraction on my record, not to mention a confrontation with a rival gang. It did not matter whether or not I did the crime. Had they arrested me under suspicion, and taken me to the police station, I would have had to prove my innocence. If I could not have proven my innocence and they stuck to their story, I would have been convicted with a law violation on my record. Even if I was not found guilty, if the Judge does not <u>*drop*</u> or <u>*dis-*</u>

miss the case, it leaves a record. These types of incidents are what causes young people to be stopped in their life's tracks before even getting started.

I had an applicant who got a ticket for looking at a police officer. Because the young man was driving a nice car (his fathers' BMW), a police officer pulled him over, frisked him and searched the car. I guess they were looking for some sort of contraband. After finding nothing, the officer arrested him for disrespecting a police officer. That applicant never did get into the Air Force. Some how he forgot to tell me about that incident during the initial interview. When I found out through my investigation, after his military entrance processing began, the Air Force considered it to be deliberately lying or in nicer terms, falsifying information, which disqualified the applicant.

You must be very careful of what you say and do, and to whom you say and do it with. Look at many of our high ranking politicians, elected officials and even television personalities. Their backgrounds are checked and rechecked so thoroughly, if they even thought wrong in their past, someone will be willing (for a fee) to blow the whistle. Many of our deceased, such as Doctor Martin Luther King Jr., Brother Malcolm X, Brother Richard Allen, President John F. Kennedy, Bruce Lee, and Elvis Presley, just to name a few, cannot even rest in peace because of something they said or did that is on record. Should you aspire to get into public service or even the public eye for that matter, your past will become your present, which can ultimately control your future.

Whether it is true or untrue, once charges have been made against you, it is permanently on your record. Look at Mike Tyson, Michael Jackson and MC Hammer. Although I am not qualified, nor do I have the facts to pass judgment on either of them, from what I do know of them, they are decent United States citizens by my standards. Yet, because of their record and charges, they are destined to drag a ball and chain placed on them by society. Fortunately for them they are financially secure. For you it may not be the case. You may have to seek traditional employment, and that is when the past becomes the present.

I remember while growing up, some of my friends used to brag about how many times they had been arrested. It was a status symbol if you had been to prison. One of my friends ended up in a foster home because his mother could not control him. Another guy bragged how he hurt the police officers and cursed them out while being arrested. Some of the guys used to play chicken with the police officers by throwing a brick or bottle at the police car. It was all a big game to give you bragging rights.

Some would describe what being in the Youth Study Center was like, with such enthusiasm. It either made you want to get arrested and find out for yourself, or do every thing possible to stay out. It was a reputation thing. The more law violations you had, the bigger the reputation you had. The bigger reputation you had, the more respect you got from the street. The more respect you got, the closer you were to being "The Man." If only there were a few fathers present, perhaps we would have had examples to show us how to be real men.

I go back to my old neighborhood as often as I can. Not so much to see what it has become, but because my mother lives there and refuses to move. The other reasons are to reflect on where I have been, where I have come from and who I am. The one thing that I always reflect on is the people I grew up with and what became of them. Many of them are either in jail or on their way back to jail. Some are strung out on drugs or dealing drugs. Some are just victims of society. Others are just trying to do the best they can to get by. The sad part is that many are dead. My mother keeps me informed on the latest deaths and fatalities.

Just recently a close friend and neighbor died from an over dose. He and I used to play roller derby when we were kids. He later got caught up in the hype of the streets and allegedly shot and killed my cousin over a one dollar bet shooting pool. He spent most of his young life trying to stay out of prison. Poetic justice? I call it a shame. He was a smart young man without a father to guide him.

The son of the man who owned the corner store just died from a drug overdose also. The bad part about it is that several years ago another son of his died from a drug overdose. And if that were not bad enough, the old man himself was killed by a blow to the head with a blunt object while trying to correct a young man who was being ungentlemanly in his store. This same old man also served in the U.S. Navy back in the sixties with my uncle. Small world . . . I just wish he had intervened with his sons more sternly when they were younger. Perhaps they would all be alive today if he had. Now his wife, daughter and other son must carry on without him, in fear of the same young man who killed their provider.

The obvious question is: why? Why would a man take another man's life? What makes a person so impervious to the pain that he inflicts it on others senselessly? Why do people commit crimes that cause their opportunities in life to fade away? Are we not being educated properly? Perhaps we are being trained and not educated at all. Perhaps it is just a conspiracy to create a larger gap between the haves and the have–nots. Perhaps the problems we are all suffering from is being perpetuated by the very people who are suppose to be stopping it. Whatever the reason, the real fact is obvious: survival of the fittest.

When contemplating law violations, you must always look past the possible infractions and ask yourself, "What will the consequences be as a result of my actions?" Some people will deliberately provoke you and later snicker that the pen is more powerful than the sword, as they sue you, take your land or property and disrupt your family. The man with the sword can cause physical harm to a person, while the man with the pen can cause harm to a nation. Think, think, think; the right thing to do is not always the best thing to do. Law violations can prevent you from becoming whatever you wish to become. So never give the so–called system the opportunity to extinguish your dreams.

5

Homosexuality

While some may consider this subject highly controversial, and would prefer to stay as far from it as they could, I prefer to deal with it straight on. No pun intended. Son, I am not a homosexual, your grandfather was not a homosexual, your great–grandfather was not a homosexual and your great–great–grandfather was not a homosexual nor was my brother Bernard a homosexual. Based on genetics and other medical DNA criteria, you are not a homosexual either. There are lots of theories on the subject of homosexuality; however, I am not an expert and I do not know anyone who is. There have been many theories, but most theories are merely justifications for what people have decided to believe.

Let Me talk about this father's feelings on a few facts. Having served over to twelve years in the military in various countries, and serving with members of all the other sister services, I firmly believe that homosexual conduct is incompatible with the traditions of the United States Military. You can state all the proof from other foreign military services substantiating that homosexual conduct is compatible with their service, and I will call your attention to all the facts that makes our great country great. If you adopt the other countries' way of running their military, then maybe you should adopt their way of life–and move.

While stationed in Germany, I recall an incident where a young heterosexual man was lured by several homosexuals to a party where they got him very drunk. They tied him up and took turns having anal sex with him. The next day, when he regained his senses and sense of feeling, he had to go to the hospital because his anal skin was split open. Needless to say, he was the talk of the base for that week. Rather than people feeling sorry for him, they made up jokes about him. This was clearly a homosexual incident and rape.

In the combat zone where instincts and split second decisions can mean the difference between life and death, you do not need to be wondering if the guy you just showered with was aroused while your back was turned. You do not need to be harboring thoughts that the guy who is supposed to be looking out for you, is busy looking at you. It is the same as being in the combat zone with women. Your mind has to be focused on the mission, or you may not return alive.

I understand that people should be mature and professional; however, I present this analogy for you to ponder. Why do females and males have to take separate showers in the military? Why can't the males just walk into the female shower with the females and act as if there is nothing wrong with it because they are professional and focused on their mission? Why can't the female just walk into the male bathroom and use the toilet because the line in the female bathroom is too long for them to wait? I am sure sexual preference has something to do with it. I would venture to say that for some homosexuals, being in the military, most definitely has its rewards.

Several homosexual friends of mines have stated their desire to enjoy the fringe benefits of communal showers in the military. They describe it as if they are having one of their fantasies fulfilled legally. They have also talked about the physical teamwork exercise in such erotic terms, the opposite sex would be accused of sexual misconduct for even speaking such tones. The opportunity to view their sexual preference regularly, is sort of like putting several monitor cameras in the bathroom or shower of the opposite sex. It is stealthily invading the privacy of another.

Now do not get me wrong and assume that I hate homosexuals. I have come to know many as close friends. It is just that the military is not for everyone. Because you are not supposed to be biased in certain decisions in the military, openly allowing homosexuals in the military would cause serious morale problems. Since that alone would take a full book just to explain, not to mention divulging classified information—which I am not prepared to do, I will leave it at that.

Homosexuals are human beings like everyone else. They live, function and operate just like you and me. Other than their sexual preference, I do not have a problem with homosexuals. One of my favorite teachers from high school was, and still is, openly a homosexual. To this day, he and I keep in touch as friends, and he is also a friend of our family. In many respects he has helped many young men and women mature into adulthood as productive heterosexual men and women.

He has demonstrated, as a role model how to stand up as a man, and do what men should do. In looking back, he has influenced me in many positive respects. Perhaps it is because he does not mix his sexual desires with his manhood. Perhaps he is more focused on helping others than pursuing others. Perhaps he is just a unique individual who has the type of wisdom that all can benefit from. Perhaps he has just never violated the trust of the people he has come to know. Whatever the reason he is the way he is, he has always had my mutual respect as a friend.

I once attended a fashion design school that seemed to be more than 50 percent homosexual. My first roommate was what we called a "Queen." That living arrangement only lasted three days. The fashion industry, at that time, was so gay that you were almost assumed gay until proven straight. I saw students turn gay like it was the plague. If you were in the closet, or the black hole for that matter, your coming out party was just around the corner. As a Disc Jockey I saw almost every type of person you thought was not homosexual, in rare form when they were on the dance floor.

One of my heterosexual (straight) friends received a job as a model for Gentlemen's Quarterly (GQ) magazine, and three months later he was unemployed because he refused to engage in homosexual activities. As a matter of fact, I quickly learned that my fashion career was going to be short lived because of three factors: I was black, I did not have lots of money, and I was not gay. Where were all the protestors then? I was discriminated against by the gay community. It seems that when you tell homosexuals they cannot do something, have something, or be something because of their sexual preference, the world is ready to prosecute you. But when heterosexuals are denied opportunities in a predominantly gay environment like the fashion industry, because they are not homosexual, they are shunned.

Speaking of shunning groups of people because of their sexual choices, many people will rely on the rulings of the church to help them understand homosexuals. I know someone who says he is a devout Christian, and he says all homosexuals should have their heads smashed by a sledge hammer. I asked him why does he say that? He said, "Because it is un–Christian like." I guess he would be considered homophobic by the gay community. To others he might be considered a good Christian. You be the judge.

Personally I know some homosexuals who attend and participate in the church regularly. They seem to be just as devoted to their religion as heterosexuals. I have devoted an entire chapter on the subject of religion so I will not attempt to discuss it here. I will say however, that everyone has religious rights and God rules everyone. As men, we are quick to judge people against our personal value systems; however, I am reminded that he among us, who is without sin, should cast the first stone. Although I have my strong feelings toward homosexuals in the military, I am not willing to throw stones.

I believe that the United States is morally ready to accept homosexuals as equal United States citizens. Besides, many of our politicians and leaders are homosexuals. However, psychologically there are individuals who will never be able to accept homosexuals. It is a form of prejudice and discrimination that makes people reject homosexuals. It is the same type of prejudice and discrimination that has continued for centuries, in spite of various amendments made to our United States Constitution.

We teach our youth and perpetuate our fears in them. It is like feeding the body. Garbage in, garbage out. You are what you eat. As with black history, we must educate ourselves and our youth on truth, and through truth we will become knowledgeable of what really happened in the past. Through knowledge we are able to discover many wonders that have been in front of our faces all the time. We just have to open our eyes.

Do not hate homosexuals. They are human beings also. Treat them as human beings. While I have and always will remain strong in my belief that men having sex with men is wrong, and women having sex with women is wrong. I understand that affection and love knows no boundaries. When two people love each other, the rest of the world does not matter to them, only the expression of their feelings. In spite of my feelings, many things that I feel are wrong will continue to go on in this world–with or without me. It is just the way it is…

6

Communication

Over the years, languages have evolved into a very complex art. There is written language, there is spoken language and there is non–verbal language. One of the most complex systems that man has invented is the art of writing. Actually art was the original form of writing, then it became complex after that. Although this chapter is not meant to be an English course, it is intended to spark your interest and to help you understand the importance of communicating in various languages and slang's.

It is said that English is one of the most difficult languages to learn, yet almost every country represented in the United Nations speak and teach English. The astonishing thing is that we as Americans, are not equally reciprocating by learning their languages as they are ours.

Although I have learned how to speak a bit of Latin, German, French, Arabic, Kiswahili, Japanese, Korean and Spanish, I have only learned how to read and write Spanish and French. I still have yet to really master any of the languages.

It is a strange feeling to be around people having a conversation in another language and not know what they are saying. You almost feel as if they are talking about you. You then begin to feel uncomfortable because you are vulnerable. That is why I recommend that everyone learn at least one other language, preferably two.

I have met people in my travels around the world that were able to speak, read and write up to six languages fluently. Talk about impressive. When you are dealing with the alphabetic letters as we know it, it is easy to accept this ability. However, when dealing with the Arabic or any of the Asian scripts, it is astonishing. I have learned how to write Arabic, and through practice, I have learned that it is not as difficult as it first appears to be. It is just like learning the American alphabet system or any type of organized system of codes for that matter. It just takes lots of practice and a sincere desire to learn.

You need to learn the languages of the countries you plan to visit, and the languages of the people you communicate with on a daily basis. In the United States, you will come in contact with people from many different countries on a daily basis; maybe even in your classes at school or working environment. It is good training to learn their language. As the world boundaries continue to grow smaller and smaller, the necessity to understand and communicate to others will grow larger and larger. Get ahead of the game and learn how to communicate with everyone.

Son, I have traveled and lived in many places other than the United States. Although I consider my English pretty good, I am constantly reminded that my English is not the only English spoken. There is a big difference between the language the Americans use and the language the British use. If you are not conscious of the differences, you

might find yourself the subject of a joke, or rather the butt of a joke.
Here are some differences.

AMERICAN	BRITISH
Apartment	Flat
Automobile	Motorcar
Checkers	Draughts
Cigarette	Fag
Crackers	Biscuits
Darts	Arrows
Elevator	Lift
Eraser	Rubber
Flashlight	Torch
French–friedpotatoes	Chips
Garbage man	Dustman
Garters	Suspenders
Gasoline	Petrol
Gearshift	Gear lever
Highway	Motor way
Hood (of a car)	Bonnet
Whore	Scrumper
Kerosene	Paraffin
Lawyer	Solicitor
Molasses	Treacle
News stand	Kiosk
Phone booth	Call box
Potato chips	Crisps
Policeman	Bobby

Prostitute	Tart
Raincoat	Mack
Station Wagon	Saloon
Subway	Underground
Suspenders	races
Thank you	Cheers
Thumbtack	Drawing pin
Truck	Lorry
Trunk (of a car)	Boot
Windshield	Windscreen

Slangs are also a part of learning various languages. Some people will disagree with this, but most of them are probably too old to remember all the slang's they used when they were growing up. How quickly we forget when the adults used to tell us that our language did not make sense, it was too radical, too foul, too strong, too vulgar, too outlandish, too vile, or not appropriate. Every generation has its language which is mis–understood by generations before theirs. In today's society (1994), if someone were to say to you, "I'm gonna have to Glock you for dissin me." You have to understand that you are about to be shot for disrespecting someone. It seems that the more languages change, the more they stay the same. Nevertheless, keeping up with slang's is not an easy thing to do.

Slangs like Ace, African, African–American, Afro, Afro–American, Afro–Centric, And you know that, Axed, B–Boy, Back, Bad, Base Line, Bastard, Beat, Beat it, Beat this, Bee Bop, Bees like that, Beg, Beggar, Big Money, Bitch, Bite This, Black, Blood, Blood Clot, Blow, Boogie, Booty Call, Booty Shaker, Bone, Box Cars, Break, Breaking, Break Dance, Brick House, Boom Box, Brain, Broth–man, Bro, Broad, Bro–Box, Brother, Burning Rubber, Burnt, But Head, Candy Man, Cat, Cheeba, Check it out, Cherry, Chick, Chill–out, Chilly–Mac, Chink, Chump, Chumpy, Clap, Clip, Clueless, Cold blooded,

Colored, Cool Breeze, Cool–out, Coon, Coon–Ass, Coke, Corn Ball, Corn Cuddy, Cotton Picking..., Crack, Cracker, Crack Head, Crew, Crib, Cuddy, Cuz, Dag, Dame, Darnet, DAZ, Deep Six, Dig it, Dime Dropper, Dirty Dozens, Dis, Dissin, Dissed, Dizam, D.J., Do That, Dog, Down–by–Law, Dope, Dope Jam, Double Dizuch, Don't Stop, Downers, Dozens, Dude, Each one teach one, Eight Ball, Eighteen and out, English, Ethnicity, Eugly, Fagot, Fair one, Far–out, Fat, Female, Fifteen Clip, Fine, Flash, Fly Girl, Fly Guy, Forty Ounce, Freak, Freaky, Freak–out, Freaky Deaky, Freeze, Fresh, Funk, Funky, Full Effect, "G", Gap, Gee, Get Busy, Get down, Get Funky, Get loose, Get lost, Get with it, G–Man, G–Money, Ghetto, Giggle, Giggle it, Gimme Five, Girlies, Glock, Go, Go Go Swing, Go Down, Golly, Golly Gee, Goodness Gracious, Gosh, Grine, Groove, Groovin, Grog, Grub, Goo Goo Gobs, Half Stepping, Hang loose, Hi Five, Hip, Hip Hop, Ho, Hoe, Hole, Hollywood, Honkey, Honkey Tonk, Hoochie–Mamma, Hood, Hoodlum, Hooters, Home–Boy, Home Girl, Homeless, Home Slice, Homey, Homo, Hot Damn, Hype, Iced, Ice Man, Illin, In effect, In the cut, In the place to be, Ink, It's all good, Izo, Jack, Jam, Jam Down, Jammy, JAP, Jigga, Jimmy, Jimmy Jawn, Jive, Joe Blow, Joe Neck Bone, Joint, Juice, Junk, Kangaroo, Kango, Kick it, Kicking it live, Kicks, King, King of..., King Pin, Knobs, Knuckle Head, Knuckle Sandwich, Later, Leg, Lips, Living for the city, Living for the weekend, Living Large, Lock–N–Load, Look–it, LOVE, Lucky Seven, Mac Daddy, Mic Check, Mix Master, Mo Money, Mom, Momma, Mother, Mothers Day, Mouth Almighty, Muda, Mug, Naa, Nerd, Neatto, New Wave, Nigga, Nigger, Nine, Nine Mill, Nocked–up, Nockers, Not the Momma, Number One, Numbers, Numbers Runner, Old–E, On, Out there, Outa here, "P", P–Funk, Packing, Paid in full, Peace, Peace Be Upon You, Peace–out, Peace–up, Peachy, Pecker, Pecker Head, Pecker Wood, Peeps, Perpetrator, Phi, Pic Nic, Piece, Pipe, Pissed off, Pop, Posse, Preach, Preemy, Pretty Boy, Preppie, Prick, Prince, Princess, Prissy, Proper, Punk, Punk Rocker, Q–Dog, Queen, Rags, Red Bone, Red Neck, Red

Skin, Right–on, Road, Rock–N–Roll, Rocks, Rockin, Rock Steady, Rubber, Sac, Scratch, Screw, Screwed, Screwed–up, Shank, Shome on, Shorty, Sike, Skank, Scallywag, Scrap, S.K.A.T., Skins, Skin tight, Slamming, Slang, Smack, Smelly, Smoke, Smooth, Snake, Snake Eyes, Snap, So Fine, Solid, Soul, Southern Baptist, Spade, Speak Easy, Spiffy, Spot, Step, Strapped, Stuck–up, Stuff, Stupid..., Suck, Swag, Swagger, Swagging, Swoop, Ten, Thacker, The Bull, There it is, Threads, Throw Down, Tired, Tit, Titty, Tit for Tat, Tizzy, Tray, Trigger Happy, True Dat, Two Faced, Uppers, Wad, Waxed, We–Funk, What's Happnin, What's sup, Whatup Wheels of Steel, White, Wighty, Word, Word–up, Work–it, "X", Yamp, Yo, Yo Baby, Yuppy, Zooted, were used and are used by so many people in so many ways, that it is almost like speaking another language.

If you were to venture to the various ghettos and listen to the slang's, you might not understand what they are talking about. If you go to Harlem, Newport News, New Hampshire, New Orleans, New Mexico, New York, Beverly Hills, North Carolina, North Dakota, North Philly, Tennessee, or any U.S. location, for that matter, you will find that while they all speak English, you will have a hard time understanding there slang's.

Technical slang and terms in various professions are just as mind boggling as geographical slang's. Listen to Lawyers, Carpenters, Mechanics, Stage Crews, Stock Brokers, Accountants, Politicians, Technicians, Cooks, Truck Drivers, Police Officers, and the one that tops them all, The Military. You will hear slang's that will go so far over your head, you might think you were listening to another language, yet it is English.

Although the list of slang words you just read is by no means complete, I never intended for it to be a complete collection of words. If you are wondering why the list is missing a lot of obvious profanity slang words, my answer is this: I purposely excluded a lot of the harsh profanity from the list because I feel it is not necessary for me to include it in this book. Some words are best left unsaid. Feel free to add yours and pass it on.

Everyone uses non–verbal languages. Most of us, however, are not conscious of our non–verbal communication messages, yet our non–verbals tell more than our verbals in many cases. Scratching your head, blinking your eyes, shifting your weight, sweating, picking your teeth, picking your nose, checking your watch, the poker face, playing with something in your hand, and of course, not looking at the person you are talking to, are all various types of non–verbal communication that sends a message. You should try and be conscious of your non–verbals to the degree that the receiver is getting the message the way you intended for it to be received. If ever you are speaking in public, it is very important to know the effects of your non–verbals. You could be a big success, or a huge flop.

Brother Malcolm X, Reverend Dr. Martin Luther King Jr., Brother Frederick Douglas, Brother Bill Cosby (a fellow Philadelphian), and Brother Arsenio Hall were and are eloquent speakers. If you listen to their messages, you are compelled to listen. Fortunately for them, they were and are also masters with their non–verbal skills as well. Imagine the President giving his inauguration speech to the world while picking his nose and constantly checking his watch. Suppose Brother Malcolm X kept his hand inside the breast of his jacket while speaking, as if he had a gun. No matter how well written his speech was, his delivery would not have been accepted as he intended for it to be. This is a very important skill that you must learn to master.

One of the most Nobel professions in the world is sales. Some may say that salesmen are made, not born. I am here to tell you that sales-men are born. "Professional" salesmen are made. Can a baby persuade a parent? Yes! Does that baby have some conscious degree of control over the parent? Yes! Try sleeping at night for eight hours straight with an infant in the house and you will learn about the little born salesman.

A salesman has to be one of the most skillful communicators in the world. He has to master many techniques, and to deal with equally skillful salesmen, he has to continue to improve his abilities or lose the sale. Not only is a salesman a skillful communicator, he can read through your non–verbals the information you did not want him to know about. It is his livelihood, and it is what he does to put food on the table.

Speaking of salesmen, I would like to help you handle a high pressure sales situation. There are two techniques a salesman uses that you have to watch out for or you will be sold. The first is to watch his lips. If his lips never stop moving, he is lying. Be careful of that one. The other technique is at the closing of the sale. This is the non–verbal one. It takes a skillful salesman to do it right. After the presentation is complete and the salesman is ready to close the sale, he will sit back in silence. He will not move his lips. He will have asked you the hard question and he will be waiting for an answer. It is the type of answer that requires you to think for a while. It is the type of answer that is usually waiting for you to sign your name. Generally at that point, whomever opens his mouth first loses. Just sit back in silence with a confident look on your face and wait until the salesman opens his mouth and speaks first. You win. He will be spewing out the answers you need to make a deal, not for him to make a sale.

When you hear the word salesman you probably think of a store, a door to door representative, or someone trying to give you something in exchange for your money. That is only one type out of hundreds. Basically, anyone communicating to others is a salesman. Looking back on history, our country was built by salesmen. The President, and any other politician for that matter, is a very good salesman. He has to be, or else he would not have gotten elected. Entertainers and orators are also salesmen. To captivate an entire audience's interest for a sustained period of time is truly an art. It is the mastering of non–verbal skills and the power of persuasion.

Son, I would like to use this paragraph to express my admiration and pride for a man whose verbal and non–verbal communication skills deserve to be recognized. As a result of his unique talents, keen sense of awareness and warm heart, he has helped more people than he will ever know. No, I am not talking about Bill Cosby, although he fits this description and then some. In stead, I am talking about someone a little younger. Brother Arsenio Hall communicates without opening his mouth, the many feelings that lay deep within his heart. Although there are many who might even be better at their craft, he is truly one to be respected for his contributions. Keep your eyes on him, and over the years you will see how communication is really an art and science. If he proves me wrong, then show him this paragraph.

In mentioning art, it is necessary for me to also speak on the art of music. Long ago, music was one of the original forms of communication. There were no telephones, mail services, telegrams, or computers at the beginning of civilization; however, there was music. The drum was one of the most widely used form of communications because it could be heard from far away. With the drum, tribes would signal for war, peace, dinner, marriages, births and even death. There were all sorts of signals and codes devised to communicate.

One of the most popular forms of communication, which has continued through all the ages, are songs. Through songs, messages are transmitted. It is through songs that we have been able to express ourselves from the heart. It was through songs that we were able to survive slavery. It was through songs that we were able to communicate to other slaves on other plantations. It was through songs such as "We Shall Overcome", that we were able to keep our heads high in a never ending struggle. It is through songs that we are able to educate our nation, while the so called educators are mis–educating us. It is also through songs that we have been able to preserve our spiritual well–being, in spite of all the adversities which surround us.

Before the Civil War, travelers to the South were struck by the singing and dancing of the slaves. It was not until late in the 19th century, however, that these songs became regarded as the Negro's first important cultural gift to America. The first spirituals were songs born of suffering. The songs tell of freedom from oppression, hard trials, wanderings in some lonesome valley, or down some unknown road, a long ways from home with brother, sister, father, mother, gone.

Today, many spirituals are sung with vigor and gusto, which serves as a way of releasing the confining pressures that African Americans know too well, and have known too long. In most cases, no one really knows who wrote these songs. They are genuine folk songs which were inspired by the people. Here is an example of one that is sometimes called: The Black National Anthem or Negro National Anthem.

LIFT EVERY VOICE AND SING
By James W. Johnson

1. Lift ev'ry voice and sing,
Till earth and heaven ring,
Ring with the harmony of liberty;
Let our rejoicing rise
High as the listening skies,
Let it resound loud as the rolling sea.

Refrain:
Sing a song, full of the faith that the dark past has taught us.
Sing a song, full of the hope that the present has brought us.
Facing the rising sun of our new day begun,
Let us march on til victory is won.

2. Stony the road we trod,
Bitter the chast'ning rod,
Built in the days when hope unborn hath died;
Yet with a steady beat,
Have not our weary feet
Come to the place which our fathers sighed?
(Refrain)

3. We have come over a way that with tears have been watered;
We have come, treading our path thro' the blood of the slaughtered
Out from the gloomy past, till now we stand at last
Where the Bright gleam of our bright star is cast.
(Refrain)

4. God of our weary years,
God of our silent tears,
Thou who hast brought us thus far on the way;
Thou who hast by Thy might,
Led us into the light,
Keep us forever in the path, we pray.
(Refrain)

5. Lest our feet stray from the places,
Our God, where we met Thee,
Lest our hearts, drunk with the wine of the world, we forget Thee
Shadowed beneath Thy hand,
May we forever stand,
True to our God, True to our native land.
(Refrain)

For many years, we have been communicating beautiful songs such as "Lift Every Voice and Sing." For many years songs like these have kept our spirits high. It is up to you to keep singing the songs for the years to come. It is up to you to continue to educate and communicate the messages of your ancestors. For it is said, "Those who do not learn from their past are doomed to repeat it."

From this chapter, I hope you have gained a deeper appreciation and curiosity for communication. It is truly one of the main ingredients that makes the world go round. Remembering that we communicate over one half of our meaning non–verbally will help you to be more conscious about how you use your body movements to enhance your message or detract from it. Mastering the nonverbal skills will also help you to project sincerity when you communicate. Your eye contact and gestures will indeed tell the receiver of your message, whether you are telling the truth or lying.

In addition to the nonverbal skills, knowing various languages and a little bit of slang may some day help you out in a pinch. As you noticed, although other countries speak English, the words do not necessarily mean the same as it does in the United States. Additionally, while we may share the United States with other citizens, through technical terms and slang's, we have created our own specialized languages; thus separating us from each other by virtue of our ability or inability to communicate.

As you go through life, you will learn more about the art of communicating. It is an art and requires a lot of time and effort to become good at it. Whether you are a singer, writer, teacher, student, businessman, politician, friend, minister, mother, father, sister or brother, your communication skills in most cases will determine the extent of your greatness.

In closing this chapter, I have chosen an excerpt from a speech on "Black Revolution" delivered in New York, April 8, 1964 by Brother Malcolm X.

"There is no system more corrupt than a system that represents itself as the example of freedom, the example of democracy, and can go all over this earth telling other people how to straighten out their house, and you have citizens of this country who have to use bullets if they want to cast a ballot. The greatest weapon the colonial powers have used in the past against our people has always been divide and conquer."

"America is a colonial power. She has colonized 22 million Afro–Americans by depriving us of first–class citizenship, by depriving us of civil rights, actually depriving us of human rights. She has not only deprived us of the right to be a citizen, she has deprived us of the right to be human beings, the right to be recognized and respected as men and women. And in this country the Black can be fifty years old and he is still a "boy."

I used this excerpt not for you to aspire to the philosophies of its meaning, rather, for you to experience how powerful communication can be.

"It is a rare man who can calm a hush upon the world while they listen to him speak." RLB

7

Problems and Struggles

Frederick Douglas once said, *"if there is no struggle, there is no progress. Those who profess to favor freedom, and yet deprecate agitation, are men who want crops without plowing the ground. They want rain without thunder and lightning. They want the ocean without the awful roar of its many waters. This struggle may be a moral one; or it may be a physical one; or it may be both moral and physical; but it must be a struggle. Power concedes nothing without demand."* He also said, *"men my not*

get all they pay for in this world, but they must certainly pay for all they get."

The struggles in the life of Frederick Douglas were more than the average human being could bare in this day and age. He struggled just to be a human being, let alone a respected human being with an identity. Even his own family treated him like an outcast. One of his greatest struggles was learning to read. Although it was against to law to teach slaves to read, he managed to find people who would teach him to read. He later learned how to write which proved to be not only a great asset to him, but to many who would follow, including you. Frederick Douglas struggled all his life, and so shall you.

Men have had to struggle for almost everything they own. Ask any millionaire or billionaire if they had to struggle for their money, and you will be educated by the answers you get. Even the ones who were fortunate enough to have been born into wealth, struggle to keep it while others are struggling to take it away from them. These sorts of struggles and problems will never go away. A very close friend once told me, "No matter what type of problems you have, you can never escape them. Even if you move, you will only exchange one set of problems for another set of problems."

Aside from extreme instances like what Mrs. Tina Turner (Annamae Bullock) went through, he was right. Speaking of Tina Turner, every day there are many women going through very similar struggles that she had to go through with her husband. My mother Annie M. (Bullock) Pompey even went through a similar situation with my brother's father. Fortunately she escaped within two years. Never beat on a woman, and never stand and watch while someone else does it. It is wrong. If a woman deserves to be beat on, that really means she needs help, not hurt.

Throughout history, men and women have struggled specifically for you and me to enjoy that which they could not. Why else would Crispus Attucks have been in battle on March 5, 1770? Why else would Harriet Tubman have risked her life 19 times to bring 300 African—

Americans to freedom with the help of the underground railroad? Why else did Rosa Parks stand her ground, which began a bus boycott. Why else did Brother Prince Hall establish the first Masonic Lodge for African–Americans? Our Forefathers and Foremothers, have built our house from the foundation up, stone by stone. It is our job to furnish that house now with the essentials that our children, our children's children and the many generations yet to come, will be able to use to continue the struggle.

As an Air Force Recruiter I would get applicants that had a tendency to disrespect our country, because of their ignorance. I would remind them that there was a military cemetery in Philadelphia with grave markers standing at attention neatly arranged in formation. I would tell them to go to that cemetery and count each grave marker one by one. I also told them that as they counted, to consider the family of each individual and how his death may have affected his family. If the applicant still did not understand the seriousness of his disrespect to our country, I would then begin to explain in morbid detail what war is like. I explained how each soldier's death was because of an oath they took so that this young applicant did not have to suffer what many in the past have suffered. By then I was usually at the point of anger from the applicant's disrespect, so I would tell him that I should smack him back in the face for the many soldiers in the grave whose face he just smacked. After that, he had two choices: Sit down and be more respectful, or get out of my office.

The struggles of a soldier, while unnoticed by many, is indeed a difficult one. Only a soldier and his family can truly understand the price such a struggle really cost. Being on call 24 hours a day, 7 days a week, 365.10 days a year, to be deployed anywhere in the world at a moment's notice so that Americans can continue to enjoy freedom and privileges that other countries cannot, is not an easy responsibility. It takes a special person to serve his country. It takes a person who is willing to struggle and make sacrifices necessary to defend our constitution and at times possibly even surrender his life for it. That is why struggles of the Buffalo Soldiers and Tuskegee Airmen should never be forgotten. For they too, are the forefathers of our country.

Beginning with the foremother, Bessie Coleman, the second African–American licensed pilot, and the first American internationally licensed pilot, struggles in aviation were always difficult. The Tuskegee Airmen were African–American aviators who battled prejudice and racism to become fighter pilots during World War II. In spite of their superior performance, innovative aero tactics, and their ability to defeat the enemy when their white counterparts could not, they were still treated as second class citizens. Nevertheless, despite staggering odds, and problems and struggles that you and I would consider unbearable, the Tuskegee Airmen rendered outstanding service to the United States of America.

Since our forefathers, our nation seems to be losing its grip on the power it once held. The younger generations for decades have been struggling to be heard. They began by hinting. Then they started asking, but the elders said, "Children should be seen and not heard." After growing tired of that reply, they started yelling. Now that the yellers are yuppies, this new generation is demanding to be heard. The struggle started long ago and has continued to grow. It is time we listened to what the younger generation has been trying to tell us over the decades.

As you grow older, never forget from whence you came and how you were. For if you do, the next generation after you will have to struggle twice as hard.

While living in Saudi Arabia as a contractor for McDonnell Douglas Services, I had the unique opportunity to be the operations director of the first Black History Month program the region of Khamis Mushayt had ever had. Living on what had been a predominantly white compound until that year, meant that there were going to be lots of struggles. Most people thought the show was going to be a failure. Some wanted it to be a failure. A few tried to make it a failure. Not only was the show a huge success, we had the participation of more than one hundred adults, children and sponsors. We controlled the weekly compound newspaper and the closed circuit television programs for the entire month. It was an astonishing accomplishment, and an enormous responsibility that somehow became a reality.

Because of our remote location and lack of funds, finding a guest speaker was not easy. I asked everyone I thought was worthy of the task and they all declined because the show had never been done before. Because of my past experience in public speaking, the program chairman, the research director and my wife conspired on me and convinced me to write a speech in case we were unable to come up with a speaker. One week before the show we had no speaker, so I began practicing.

When the night of the show finally arrived, I was the guest speaker. At the age of 30 I felt I did not have enough gray hairs to deliver the speech. As a matter of fact I had no gray hairs at all. I was not nervous because I had to do a speech. I have done many in my time. I was nervous because I was about to make history. I was about to continue the struggle in front of people who knew more than I did about the very subject I was going to speak on. Nevertheless, my elders gave me encouragement and I went on stage with pride. Because of its value, I would like to share that speech with you:

"We Shall overcome someday"... *That was the slogan and that was the dream of not only Dr. Martin Luther King Jr. but for many of our African descendants of yesterday. I often wonder if they were alive today to see the fruits of their labor, the results of their blood shed and the aftermath of their death, what would they tell us, what would they tell us that would enkindle us for tomorrow.*

What would they tell us if they knew that many of us have forgotten our past? What would they tell us if they knew that many of us have no idea where we came from, let alone who we are? Indeed we have become comfortably complacent with the luxuries that modern science and technology have given us. Being here in Saudi Arabia has even given most of us financial opportunities that many of our families and friends back home only dream about.

And let's not fool ourselves. Financial freedom is a good feeling . . . However, are you fooling yourself into thinking that all your wealth, all your happiness and all your success are all the fruits from your own labor? For those of you who really feel that way about yourself, I am here to tell you that such is not the case. Our Forefathers and Foremothers survived whips, chains, dog bites, disease, high pressure water hoses, night sticks, starvation, humiliation, degradation, and segregation because they had vision, they had foresight, and most of all they had courage. They knew within their hearts that someday the fruits of their labor would overcome the inhumane atrocities they were forced to struggle with.

Our African descendants knew that the fruits of their labor would truly reap the benefits as a result of their bloodshed. In your programs you will find the meaning of red, black and green on page 14. It alludes to the red standing for the blood and the struggle of our people. What is not there, however, is the true meaning of the red. For you cannot write, indent, print, stamp, stain, hue, cut, carve, mark or engrave the true meaning of red on anything movable or immovable. The true meaning of red lies within the deoxyribonucleic acid; better known as the DNA structure. DNA continues to carbon copy the blueprint of our ancestors within us all. Although their blood may have been shed, it still runs through my veins. We are all repositories of the wisdom, the strength, and the beauty of kings, queens, and potentates. We possess the same blueprints that made inventors courageous; philosopher's thinkers; scientist— geniuses; and dreamer's explorers.

Within us lies the fortitude to withstand the physical abuse that continues to plague us even today; as with the Rodney King incident in California. Within us lies the temperance to look past the racism, prejudice, and ignorance so that we can succeed in spite of the negative personalities we are forced to live with. Within us lies the prudence to be responsible and to do the right thing, as well as the justice to build strong families and great nations, under firm leadership. However, just like any other blueprint, just like any other design you lay down on the blue print for yourself, you must study it, analyze it, and learn it before you can begin to work. You must educate yourself about yourself, then use yourself to better yourself so that ultimately, you can be yourself. And as you learn about yourself and who you are, you will also learn that nothing in life is free. Everything has a price.

So tonight I ask you all, how are you living? Do you do unto others as you would have them, do unto you? Will your children be proud of you and your accomplishments after you are gone? Yes, the children are our future; teach them well and let them lead the way. But ask yourself, have you done the very same things that you are demanding of them to do? Have you challenged yourself to be better? Have you taken advantage of various educational opportunities to enrich yourself and your family? Are you planning for a better tomorrow and achieving your goals, or are you just talking? And for that talker, are you talking about your neighbor and friends? Are you talking about your brother and sister while trying to prevent them from achieving because you have chosen not to?

Indeed, we all have opportunities to be whomever or whatever we want to be. Some of us just do not know how to play the game called life. The game of life is just like any other game. There are rules to follow. Players to challenge you, and the object is to win. Take basketball for instance. The object is to shoot the ball into the basket. The struggle is that the other team is trying to stop you. Now you could walk off the court crying and sobbing to your coach about all the obstacles that are in your way; or you could score anyway. You can score in spite of the obstacles in front of you trying to block your shots, trying to keep you from scoring and getting ahead in life. The choice is yours.

What I have said this evening was not specifically directed to the African-American, rather to all descendants of the Negroid, the Mongoloid, the Caucasoid, and the Asian. Each of us is a descendant of our ancestors; from one race: the Human Race.

It seems that every time I read that speech, it touches me and commands me to think. I hope it does the same for you. No matter who you are, where you are or how you live, there will always be obstacles to deal with and struggles to challenge you. As a man, it is your responsibility to learn to deal with these obstacles and struggles.

From the time you were a baby you have had to struggle. Just being born was a struggle for you and your mother. Growing up with many of life's challenges is a struggle in itself. The struggles that you have faced and will face are like your own shadow. It has always been there and will always be there. You may not be able to always see it, but it is there waiting for you. And when you finally turn around and confront your struggles, just remember what Frederick (Bailey) Douglas used to say. *"If there is no struggle, there is no progress."*

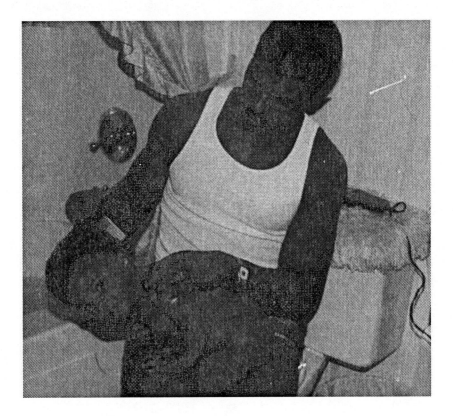

8

Friendship

Emerson once said, "A friend may well be reckoned the masterpiece of nature." He also said, "The only way to have a friend is to be one." Son, I wish I could tell you how to know when you have found a friend. In my travels throughout the world, I have met well over tens of thousands of people. I have shaken hands and looked eye ball to eye ball with people I cannot even remember. I have worked with thousands of people and it is hard sometimes to even remember what they look like. I send out more than 100 Christmas cards every year and I never receive even half back in reply. I cannot even remember all the names of the many so–called friends I grew up with. Some were even short term girlfriends. When it comes to friends, I sometimes ask people to think about all the classmates and friends they have had from first grade to the last day of high school or college and tell me how many they keep in touch with as friends. Even they are surprised when they begin to try and recall the faces.

I have no real definition or philosophy on friendship. I do have a couple of true friends and several whom are close, but not as close as my true friends. My true friends will do almost anything I ask them to do without question. Whether it is financially, morally, spiritually, emotionally, they are there and will always be there. If I should be out of communication with them for ten years, the friendship continues to grow. And when we finally meet or communicate, it is like a continuation of yesterday. Equally, I am willing to do whatever they ask of me. I will even risk my life for a true friend.

Do you truly feel that you are your brother's keeper? Do you truly want for your brother that which you want for yourself? While I could go on and on, I could never really convey to you what friendship is all about. It is a feeling which cannot be expressed in words. Although you and that true friend may have never established that title verbally, without even saying anything, you know.

I caution you to never search for friendship, allow it to evolve. Trust no one because they are your friend, rather because they earned your trust. As for secrets . . . I learned in the military, the best way to keep a secret is not to tell anyone. Do not tell a soul. If you do, it is no longer a secret, it is news.

Son, I would like to also mention, that while I may have a couple of true friends, they are also human. They are also capable of making mistakes. In most cases you will forgive a friend for making a mistake. You will do almost anything to preserve the friendship. You will even trust them. To put your trust in someone is a dangerous thing. When you trust someone, you are giving them a part of you. If the trust is ever violated, you lose that part of you. Should you ever be betrayed by someone you considered your friend, you will see a side of you that you never knew existed. You may even scare yourself.

Once I had a very good friend whom I grew to trust. He was my right hand in a business I owned called Third Dimension Sound. Although he was not always on time, he was otherwise dependable. He did whatever I asked him to do and I took care of him as best as I could. One day he got married. Although I was excited for him getting married, I was not excited about his choice.

The same year he got married, my wife and I had to relocate from Hampton, Virginia to Philadelphia due to a career progression. Because he was such a close friend and because he had just got married and his wife was due to have a baby, and because his financial status was not where he would have liked it to be, I offered to let him rent my newly rebuilt, completely renovated house. Why not, after all, he did help me with some of the renovations. As a matter of fact, I offered to rent it to him for half the mortgage because of his financial status. We agreed with a handshake. (Big mistake).

At first, he was only paying about a week late. Next, he was about three weeks behind. Since I was now in Philadelphia and could not talk to him face to face, I called him and asked about the money. He told me it was in the mail. It was; just not all of it. This went on for several months. Mind you, he was only paying half the mortgage, which meant I had to pay the other half. After a while, I got tired of paying the entire mortgage for him and his family to live, and paying my expenses in Philadelphia for me and my family to live; not to mention I was struggling to make it in life like everyone else.

I called him and asked him what was the problem. I found out he had given his wife the responsibility of paying the bills and he thought I was receiving the money that he gave her to send me. When he told me that, I lost it. I cursed him out so bad, to this day I still feel sorry for the things I said to him. Since I could not physically express my feelings on him, I hurt his feelings as painfully as I could on the telephone. I gave him one week to vacate my property and told him that anything left in the house after that week was mine. I also told him that if after one week he was found on my property, he would be considered trespassing. After hanging up the phone I cried. I loved this man as if he were my brother, and it hurt to have to put him out.

I hope one day he and I will meet face to face and resolve our differences. We lost contact after he moved out. I still consider him a friend, but you have to be careful who you trust. Because the change in our relationship was after his marriage, I am willing to give him the benefit of the doubt. Had it happened straight from him, I would have treated him like an enemy.

Speaking of marriages, having been in the military, I have seen all sorts of marriages come and go. I have seen people marry natives from so many countries and not even be able to communicate, because of the language differences. I have also seen where a spouse from another country was the best thing that ever happened to some people. I am constantly surprised at the divorce rate and second and third marriages I see from the military. One of my true friends has just married for the third time. I have to give him credit. I think his first wife lasted six or seven months and his second wife lasted two or three months. As soon as he realized his mistake, he corrected it. I think one took some money from him and tried to steal his car or something to that effect. I am not sure about the other one. Oh well, he is married now for the third time, so we will see what happens.

It is not easy choosing a spouse to spend the rest of your life with. Look at the divorce rates. That tells you how well people are at making decisions. When it comes to a house, people spend hours of research, consult all sorts of professionals, surf the Internet, contemplate for a while, narrow the choices down from several, then make their decision. When it comes to a spouse, you should do more than that; however, most people do not. Marriage is truly one of the biggest decisions and investments you will ever make, and if you ask people to tell you how they met and married, you will get all sorts of interesting stories.

In my case, it was also interesting. I was attending Fashion Institute of Technology in New York, majoring in Menswear Design and Marketing. Somewhere around December 5th, 1981 at about 5pm on a Sunday, I was working on a term project in the design lab. While working on my project a pretty young lady whom I had never seen before, walked into the room and started talking to my friend. After a few minutes went by, I asked my friend if he was going to introduce me to his friend. He did. Because I was a well–known Disc Jockey in the city, I asked if she ever heard of me. Of course she said, "No!" That hurt my ego. After a few more questions, I asked her what was she doing at the school on a Sunday night? She replied she was looking for a typewriter to do a final term paper.

Because there were no classes or labs with typewriters open at that hour on a Sunday evening, I offered to allow her the use of my typewriter. I told her that since I had an apartment right across the street from school it was no imposition. She agreed, and we left. While she typed, I cooked dinner. I made her take a break for dinner and after dinner she went straight back to her work. When she finished, we talked for a few minutes and exchanged numbers in case she needed a typewriter again. She then called the limousine service for a ride, and went home.

The next day, I called her and she asked if she could use my typewriter again. That was the beginning of a beautiful relationship. A few weeks later, she dissolved the relationship with her boyfriend and I gave up my relationships as well. We were inseparable. A very close friend called it "sickening love." We did not have a care in the world other than each other.

Shortly after we met, I found out I had passed the entrance exam (Armed Service Vocational Aptitude Battery) for the Air Force. That meant I had to leave New York in March to prepare for Air Force Basic

Training in May. Because I wanted my (then) girlfriend to finish school, I made a deal with her. I told here that after going through all the training and ending up wherever in the world I may end up, if the relationship is still strong, I may marry her.

I completed my four months of training and ended up in Germany. Throughout the entire separation we wrote each other almost every day. I would send 20 birthday cards, fifteen Christmas cards, 20 valentines' day cards, all sorts of other cards, letter tapes, regular letters almost every day and lots of packages. We communicated almost every day by correspondence, for more than two years–thanks to the U.S. Postal service.

In December 1983 she and my mother flew to Germany to visit me. Mom stayed for three weeks and Esther stayed for six. On Christmas Eve, I proposed to her and we became engaged. We took our engagement honeymoon in Paris on New Years Eve. She later went back to New York and secured a position as a Textiles Designer. In March 1984 I went home on emergency leave because my grandfather was dying. She came to Philadelphia to be with me.

After the funeral I told my mother (jokingly) we were going to get married while I was home. Since economically, in the military, I would get an extreme increase in pay if I was married, this would have allowed us to save more for our home furnishings. Of course, Mom did not believe me, so we did it. In a few days we were married. We contacted all the immediate family for their blessings, prepared all the logistics and did it. Since there was a family bus trip leaving from the church we were getting married in, we decided to wait until the bus left and allow the minister to marry us in private. It would not have been fair to have only one half of the family there, so we elected not to have any of the family present. However, we would have a reception months later when I returned back to the Unites States permanently. In September, after my Germany tour of duty was completed, we held the best outdoor reception Southampton Long Island has ever seen. We still talk about how much fun we had that day and night. What a party…

That is the story of how we got married. We were very good friends first, we fell in love afterwards, we tested the love with time and distance, then we made a promise to each other.

I cannot tell you how to select the right person, but I can say this. I married one of my true friends. My wife knows almost everything about me, and in spite of myself, she still loves me. That is friendship.

Defining friendship and describing friendship is not an easy thing to do. Through this chapter I have tried to convey to you not only the meaning of friendship and how it evolves, but some of the dangers and hazards that can occur. Through my experiences perhaps you will be able to see a couple of your mistakes before you make them, thus bypassing those errors. Keep in mind that not everyone who tries to be your friend, is a friend. Sometimes people use the term friendship in order to use you. They play on your feelings until they have control over you through your feelings.

Conversely, when you are not even looking, or not even trying to find a friend, there you have it. A friend for life who will stick with you through thick and thin. When that happens, you will know. You will understand the mutual responsibility that you have in maintaining the trust and respect that is required of true friends. It may not be easy, but it is sure worth it as the year's pass by.

I cannot remember where I acquired this poem from, but I think it is worth passing on to you.

An old man once said:
"I've come to know, as I grow old,
That friends are worth their weight in gold,
And that a handclasp and a smile
Are things that make this life worthwhile."

"Likewise I find, as life speeds by,
That treasures in my friendships lie;
And all the money, in the end,
Can scarce compare to one kind friend!"

9

Religion

In the name of Allah, Most Gracious, Most Merciful. Praise be to Allah The Cherisher and Sustainer of the Worlds: Most Gracious, Most Merciful; Master of the Day of Judgement. Thee do we worship, and Thine aid we seek. Show us the straight way, The way of those on whom Thou has bestowed Thy Grace, Those whose (portion) Is not wrath. And who go not astray. (The Holy Qur–an, Surat Al–Fatiha 1, Ayat 1–7)

In the beginning God created the heavens and earth. The earth was without form and void; and darkness was on the face of the deep. And the spirit of God was hovering over the face of the waters. Then God said, "Let there be light"; and there was light. And God saw the light, that it was good; and God divided the light from the darkness. God called the light Day, and the darkness He called Night. So the evening and the morning were the first day. Then God said, "Let there be a firmament in the midst of the waters, and let it divide the waters from the waters." Thus God made the firmament, and divided the waters which were above the firmament; and it was so. (The Holy Bible, Genesis, Chapter 1, Verses 1–7)

The first seven Ayats of the first Surat in the Holy Qur–an begin as a prayer. The first seven verses of the first chapter in the Holy Bible begin as creation. It is known to all men of the craft; before entering upon any great or important undertaking, we should always invoke the aid of Deity.

The subject of religion is probably the most controversial subject in the world, and has been for a long time. The root of most religions is supposed to be, belief in a divine creator and ruler of the universe. The goal of most religions seems to be peace, yet it seems that nearly all the wars and battles of this world where fought in the name of, or because of, religion. Look at the state of the world today and why it is the way it is. Religion . . .

There will come a time in your life when you will become curious about religions. You may already be of one faith or denomination when that time comes. You may even change your religion more than once. It happens . . . In the final analysis, you must be comfortable with whatever religion you choose. You must not only understand your religion, you should challenge it every day. If the religion is able to stand the test of time, it should certainly be able to stand any test you come up with. On that premise, allow me to share with you a bit of my journey in search of truth.

I was born and raised in what some call a Southern Baptist family. As a young boy, my brother and I would visit our grandparents in North Carolina during the summer to help out on the farm and give my mother a break from us. I remember picking cucumbers from sun up to sun down. I remember plowing the field with a mule, or rather it dragging me behind it. I recall that old pick up truck my grandfather used to wheel with his one whole arm and the other nub. Some time ago he had got his hand cut off. I think it happened in the saw mill. I remember him beating my brother and me with a switch with that one good arm when we misbehaved.

I also remember we would go to church three to four times a week for one thing or another. Sometimes we would go for service, sometimes for rehearsals and sometimes because my grandparents had meetings. Those days are truly memorable experiences I look back on now with pride and respect.

In Philadelphia during my second to fourth grade school years, we used to go to a day care center after school, run by a church in a church, until my mother picked us up after she got off work. Later in Philadelphia, around the age of 10 or so, my mother used to send my brother and me to Baptist Sunday school. This was the beginning of my search for truth.

We were on the track team for the church, we sang, we acted in the Easter play and we learned Bible verses. We also observed the elders when they were drinking and flirting. We would hear them use profanity and say other things that were not so nice. I began to wonder why my brother and I had to go to church. We would walk about a mile, sometimes in the rain or snow on some days just to go to church. After awhile we started going to the store and buying something for ourselves with the quarter we were given for the collection plate from my mother. Since she did not go with us to church, we would also go to the park and play basketball sometimes instead of going to church. I do not think my mother ever knew we played hooky from church to play basketball. After a while, my brother and I could not see the point in going to church, so we stopped.

Now do not get me wrong and feel that I hate church or Mom does not like it. On the contrary, I enjoy going to church. I have grown to enjoy listening to and watching preachers as they perform their sermons. I also enjoy the gospel music and singing, with the exception of some of the Jesus parts which I will get to later. Church has been, and probably will always be, a platform for many people to become more than they ever would have been without it. Some of the best singers have come from the church. Some of the best musicians have also come from the church. Some of our most eloquent speakers began practicing in the church. Several members of our family have also recorded music, produced gospel videos, written jingles for gospel radio stations, and even performed in plays such as God is trying to tell you something. For many reasons, we need to be thankful for the church.

Since my youthful years, my mother has been very active in the church and in the assistance of its members and still is. She has been instrumental in helping senior citizens, organizing trips, fund raisers, and filling in wherever she is needed. For several years she also served as the church clerk which was a task that was not easy. Indeed Mom has been a pillar in her church.

Church has also been there for many families. As a matter of fact son, you and your sister were christened in a church. Your mother and I were married in that church and my Grandfather and Brother had their funeral services performed at that same church. Churches have been there for families in times of need when the government was too busy thumbing through their book of excuses. Churches were very instrumental in helping slaves survive, abolishing slavery and establishing equality. Look at all the outstanding men of today with the letter's Rev. in front of their names. We owe a great deal of gratitude for their services.

When I was a teenager, several of my friends began going to church. Some because they were really sincere, and others because they thought it was hip and they could pick up girls. Every once in a while they would convince me to go. I went to Jehovah Witness Kingdom Halls, Jewish Synagogues, Catholic Cathedrals, and all sorts of other Christian Churches. It was a cultural experience to say the least. Every once in a while I would get the nerve to ask questions.

I would ask questions like where did God come from? Why were we living in poverty while others were living very well? Who wrote the bible and why? Why were there so many versions instead of the original? What color was Jesus? How can people paint pictures of the last supper if no one was there? How is it that we know everything that God did all the way at the beginning when no one was there? Where else in the universe was there life that God was looking out for as he was us? I began to become obsessed with these questions I had rolling around in my head because most people could not answer them satisfactorily. As I grew older, my curiosity became stronger and my journey and quest for truth had begun.

Since then, I have learned that most people who call themselves religious, including the ministers, preachers, or whomever thinks they are qualified to disseminate the information of the holy book; generally are not as educated about the subject as they think they are. Most people have not read the book they are partial to. Most people have not even researched the chapter they are talking about. There are only a few who can truly dissect their particular religious book and explain its real contents.

Because the Bible was such a universal book, and the one I grew up with, I decided to challenge it. I decided to begin with the phrase, the Father, the Son and the Holy Spirit. Are they the same, are they separate, are they all God or are they independent? While people are quick to give you answers off the top of their heads, the Bible cannot substantiate all their sayings. This confused me, so I began to study more. As I studied, I learned the premise for Christianity was a take off from the word Christ, as in Jesus Christ. Since Jesus was sent to save the Jews, and their language back then was different from the words we use today, I decided to try and find out Jesus' real name and how it came to be. The search was a difficult one, and I still am not satisfied with my findings. So, I challenge you to attempt to do better than I have in a search for the original name of Jesus Christ.

I looked up the origin of <u>Christ</u> and was referred to <u>cream</u>. The origin of <u>cream</u> said, this word had originally no connection with cows or milk. It is first, from AS. <u>crisma</u>, from OFr. <u>cresme</u>, from L. <u>chrisma</u>, consecrated oil, used in anointing, from Gr. <u>chrisma</u>, anointing, from <u>chriein</u>, to anoint. The <u>Christ</u> is the anointed one, Gr. <u>Cristos</u>—hence christen, Chistian, Christmas. I next studied the origin of annoint, it referred me to lotion. This was a dead end because the origin of lotion kept referring to bathing and washing.

Not being satisfied with my findings, I began talking to so–called scholars on the subject of Jesus. There were as many answers as there were scholars. After their frustration of searching for answers to my questions and not being able to substantiate all of their answers with references. I was told that Jesus was sent as the Messiah. I researched Messiah... It sent me to criss–cross. In my studies of criss–cross, I was surprised at what I learned. The alphabet, in the medieval hornbook, was preceded by a cross; thus it made the Christ–cross row. The reduplicative tendency of tongues changed this to criss–cross, which no longer need be the religious cross. Christ is L. from Gr. Christos; cp. cream. Similarly Messiah is from Aram. mshiha, from Heb. mashiah, from mashah, to anoint. cp. conjure.

Cross is from AS. cros, from L. crux, cruci, whence Eng. crucify, to make into a cross. The meaning of the adjective is from the opposite directions of the two sticks; hence, also, across, from AS. a, on + cross. Hence, to be at cross–purpose; and cross angry.

Although I have researched the word conjure and found it to be a valuable piece to the puzzle, this book is not meant to be an encyclopedia or a dictionary of religion, so I will conclude this particular road map type research by giving you an abbreviation translation to the word origins. AFr... Anglo–French; AS... Anglo–Saxon; cp...compare; Eng...English; Gr...Greek; L...Latin; OFr...Old French.

I included this brief portion of my research to demonstrate to you several things. First, none of those definitions said anything remotely similar to God. Second, I wanted to show you that the translations and transliterations over the years have distorted many words from their original meaning. Third, although Jesus was said to have been born in Bethlehem, many of the words in the Bible are of Latin, Greek, French, and Anglo–Saxon origin. If the search for truth in the origin of Christ was so extensive for me, and I still am not satisfied with all my results, imagine how distorted from the truth other words in the Bible may be.

To assist you with some sort of starting point in trying to prove or disprove whether or not Jesus is God, I will give you some references from several books, chapters and verses for you to read for yourself and begin your studies.

Acts 2:22; Revelation 19:10; John 12:49; John 5:30–31; John 14:28; John 17:3; John 13:16; John 20:17; Mark 13:32; John 8:40. Look these verses up and you will be surprised at what you read. Most are the words of Jesus himself.

After being both surprised and relieved at what I was finding, the answers to many of my questions started to reveal themselves. I began to ask myself many questions. Then I tried to find out the answers myself.

Consider Genesis 9:25, 1 Timothy 6:1, and Titus 2:9 and imagine, how could the scriptures possibly preach racism and discrimination?

Consider distortions in verses from 2 King 24:8 and 2 Chronicles 36:9 and say: how can the faith be based on the distorted scriptures? Was he eight, or eighteen? Ask a minister. I will show you more slight distortions shortly.

Note Matthew 10:35 and say: how could the truth and divine scriptures preach hatred between man and his family? If you really want to be enlightened, try reading all the verses in chapter 10, especially verse 34.

Another question I had was about the King James Version of the Bible and the New International Version (NIV). While they both carry obvious differences in meanings, which particular version of these two may be taken as standard?

In the light of Matthew 15:25, Jesus came only for the people of Israel, so how could the message of Jesus be taken as universal?

Consider Mark 12:29 and Mark 14:36–37 which indicates Jesus had normal human feelings and emotions, how could a man with normal human instincts be God?

According to the Bible, Hebrews 7:1–3, Melchisedec came to existence without a father and mother. And before him, Adam was created
without a father or mother. In spite of this, none of them have been
taken as God. How could Jesus who was born without a father, be
taken as a God or son of God merely because of his unique birth?

In my research I have read that the Bible contains close to 50,000
errors. No that is not a misprint. I said, close to Fifty Thousand errors.
I am not a religious scholar nor a literary master so I cannot point them
all out to you, therefore I am not sure how accurate that statement may
be. I will however, give you several references from the old and new testament that you may compare. The differences between the two com-
parisons should help to spark your own questions. After looking up the
few I give you, consider that there might still be over 49,000 errors left.

I have already given you 2 Kings 24:8 and 2 Chronicles 36:9. If you
did read it already and you have a reference type Bible, you will notice
that even in the Bible, 2 Chronicles 36:9 referred you to 2 Kings 24:8.
What it fails to do is discredit the one that is false so that you may
know the truth. If you will compare 2 Samuel 8:4 to 1 Chronicles
18:4; Matthew 26:34 to Mark 14:30; Acts 9:7 to Acts 22:9; and finally
King James Version, Acts 22:9 and New International Version Acts
22.9 you will be well on your way to really learning the Bible.

My final question, which has puzzled me my entire life, is what
color was Jesus? Some say it does not matter. To them I say you are lost
in the wilderness. Why would the majority of churches display all sorts
of pictures, sculptures and other relief's of Jesus for the world to see if it
does not matter? Although the Bible says: God Said, "You shall have
no other gods before Me. You shall not make for yourself any carved
image, or any likeness of anything that is in heaven above or that is in
the earth beneath, or that is in the water under the earth; you shall not
bow down to them nor serve them. For I, the Lord your God, am a
jealous God, visiting the iniquity of the fathers on the children to the
third and fourth generations of those who hate Me, but showing mercy

to thousands, to those who love Me and keep My commandments."
Exodus 20:3–6.

People of the Bible continue to ignore messages that are not conve-
nient to their bank accounts. These were God's words, not Jesus. To
the card companies, painters, designers, advertisers, ministers, book
stores and all the other money making entities, it does matter. If it
matters to them, it most certainly matters to me.

I am not going to tell you the answer. I will spark your curiosity by
saying that if Jesus is not the image that the world has caused us to
believe, then all who believe the myth have been living a lie. There is a
movie called Jesus Christ Superstar and others, where they depict the
typical image of what we have come to be familiar with as the image of
Jesus. To watch the mental state of a person change in reverence, simply because they are looking at a long haired person in a white robe is a
remarkable thing. However, suppose they are worshiping the wrong
figure. Suppose the world was to have to destroy all the images and figures of Jesus as we know it and replace them all with a different one.
That in itself would probably cause another war somewhere.

I could go on and on, but instead I will allow you to pick up where I
left off. Consider the scriptures Ezekiel 1:27 and 8:2; Daniel 7:9; Revelation 1:14–15. Those scriptures will give you a clue as to what he
looks like. Matthew 1:1–16 and Luke 3:23–38 will give you his genea-
logical information. From tracing his roots and their tribal origin, you
should be able to answer the question of color. Should you find out
that he is not what we are lead to believe, then ask yourself the real
challenging question. Why...?

Speaking of asking the question why? Why are many religious fol-
lowers so quick to degrade other religions? Many of the religions they
degrade are very similar to their own, yet they denounce anything that
is not what they practice. This is wrong.

The religion of Islam is different from Christianity and in many
respects very similar. As with any religion, it is the choice of the person
whether or not he follows his book. Most people are familiar with the

fact that Muslims do not eat pork. Some will even tease Muslims because of their observance of the Qur–an. The odd thing is that the Bible also regards pork as forbidden. While some people will be quick to point out Genesis 1:30 and 9:3 in their defense. That statement is merely a general statement. To find out the specifics, you must also consider Genesis 1:29; Leviticus 11:1–8 with special attention to verses 7–8; Isaiah 65:2–5 with special attention to verse 4. Isaiah 66:15–17. Coming from a southern family background, I have eaten all types of pork. My mother made sure I always had chitterlings on Christmas. Ham hocks and collard greens would snatch me by the nose from wherever I was. I liked the food my mother cooked. It was good. It was Mom's cooking. The question I am faced with as an adult is, do I listen to Mom, or do I listen to Mom's book and the medical professionals?

The microscope has revealed that the flesh of the hogs is often infested with trichina worms, which when taken into the human body, multiply and begin to work their way through the entire system, even into the brain and heart. This condition is known as trichinosis. Thus far there is no known cure for the disease, since nothing has been discovered which will kill the trichina without killing the person, once the worms have started working into the flesh.

According to the <u>Illinois Health Messenger</u> the microscopic examination of meat was considered by the government, years ago, as impractical: Several years ago the government abandoned the microscopic examinations of meat as impractical, so that meats are no longer certified as free from trichina.

It is possible to find a half–million trichinae to a single pound of muscle... The worms enter the human digestive tract as tiny, almost invisible cysts which digest and release the worms so that they burrow through the walls of the stomach or duodenum to the blood stream. Eventually, these little guys can be fatal. If the medical profession says to stay away from it and the various holy scriptures say to stay away from it, what should you do?

Another similarity is the manner of prayer. Here again some Muslims are teased because of the manner in which they pray. If others would study the bible, they will find that ABRAHAM, Genesis 17:3; JOSHUA, Joshua 5:14; MOSES AND AARON; Numbers 16:20–22; JESUS, Matthew 26:39 and Mark 14:35, all fell on their face and prayed. I would like to remind you that the Lord's prayer starts off, "OUR FATHER." Jesus did not pray to himself, he prayed to God. How do you pray?

Son, by now you may be asking yourself what is the best religion? What religion should you choose? I cannot answer that question for you. Only you can make that choice. I will tell you that I believe in God. I believe in a Supreme Architect of this Universe. I am what I like to consider myself to be, a righteous person. I believe in good and truth. If it is good and true, then it is for me.

For over ten years I have been learning about the religion of Islam. Living in Saudi Arabia has given me privileges to study first hand from some generous scholars. Since Islamic Law is the law of the land, my Saudi friends have provided me with extensive information on their ways of life. Going to Mecca and performing Umra was one of the most memorable religious experiences I have ever felt. Because of all my research and experience over the years, I have learned a lot about Christianity and Islam as it relates to me. The one thing I would like to pass on is that no religion made by man is perfect. They all have their flaws. Only God is perfect, and there is only one God.

The Arabic word Islam means peace, submission and obedience. The religion of Islam is the complete acceptance of the teachings and guidance of God, as revealed to His Prophet Muhammad (PBUH). A Muslim is one who believes in God and strives for total reorganization of his life according to His revealed guidance and the sayings of the Prophet. He also works for building human society on the same basis. "Muhammadanism" is a misnomer for Islam and offends its very spirit. The word "Allah" is the proper name of God in Arabic. It is a unique term because it has no plural or feminine gender.

Islam is not a new religion. It is, in essence, the same message and guidance which Allah revealed to all Prophets: Say, we believe in Allah and that which has been revealed to Abraham and Ishmael and Isaac and Jacob and the tribes and that which was given to Moses and Jesus and to other Prophets, from their lord. We make no distinction between any of them, and to him we submit. (Qur–an 3:84)

You may contemplate from time to time about some of the holidays that we as Americans celebrate. The name holiday comes from the two words Holy Day. Christmas is one of those holidays people have come to accept as when Jesus Christ was born. There are all sorts of stories and legends surrounding the origin of this particular holiday. Do you have any idea why people use "Xmas," instead of "Christmas?" It is not a modern abbreviation. It originated with early Greek Christians in the second and third centuries <u>A.D.</u> In Greek, the letter <u>chi</u>, which is printed as an X, is the first letter of Christ's name. The X itself was often used as a sacred symbol because it resembled the Holy Cross, and many large X's can still be seen on the walls of Roman catacombs where they were drawn as symbols of Christ and the Crucifixion.

The practice of exchanging presents at Christmas originated with the Romans. Every December, the Romans celebrated a holiday called the Saturnalia. During this time the people gave each other good–luck presents of fruit, sweets, pastry, or gold. When the Christians began to celebrate their own holiday at this time of year, they simply took over the tradition.

Did you know that Christmas was once illegal in England? In 1643 the Puritans outlawed all Christmas celebrations, banned the keeping of Christmas trees, and made the singing of Christmas carols a crime. These laws were maintained until the Restoration. Many Puritans in New England also adhered to these regulations, curtailing Christmas festivities to such a degree that even the making of mince pies was forbidden.

Throughout history, nearly all religions of the world have had a celebration that falls close to Christmas. In Judaism it is Chanukah, the

Festival of Lights. Pre–Christian Scandinavians enjoyed the Feast of the Frost King. In Rome there was the Saturnalia, in Egypt the mid-winter festival in honor of the god Horus. The Druids had an annual mistletoe–cutting ceremony. Mithraists celebrated the feast of Sol Invictus, representing the victory of light over darkness. In Hinduism the feasts of Diwali and Taipongal are observed close to the Christmas season.

In the United States we celebrate Kwanzaa, which means "the first" or "the first fruits of the harvest," in the East African language of Kiswahili. Kwanzaa is a unique American Holiday that pays tribute to the rich cultural roots of Americans of African ancestry. Kwanzaa is observed from December 26th through January 1st. Kwanzaa was founded in 1966 by Dr. Maulana Karenga, a Black Studies professor who describes himself as a cultural nationalist. Kwanzaa originated as a cultural idea and an expression of the nationalist Us organization which was headed by Dr. Karenga.

Although many other civilizations have similar festivals, those are just a few to give you some background on Christmas. I will say that I do celebrate the Christmas holiday. Not so much for its religious tone, but because it has grown to be a traditional family celebration.

Some of the meanings attached to the season, such as good will toward men, sharing, peace on earth, and others are particularly emphasized during this time of the year–which is good. Giving and receiving gifts is always fun. Sharing moments and memories with the family also establishes a special feeling. These are all traditions surrounding the season. As you get older, you will be able to reflect on the fond memories you had as a child. These memories are what makes Christmas what it is to me. A wonderful tradition which comes only once a year to add to your memories of a life time.

Son, I have tried to give you enough information for you to maintain your own identity. As stated earlier, many dangers have been caused in the name of and because of religions. Be careful of cults and evangelists. Blind faith is no faith. God has given you a brain, so use it.

In closing this very important chapter of religion. I have been given permission by Dr. Ahmad Dawood Al–Mizjaji to share with you a piece of knowledge he has given me.

"The ability to think, reason out and decide is a great blessing for the human mind. For reasoning, there is a need to have real facts and an unprejudiced mind. In vital issues, the basic elements of real facts and a mind free of prejudice assume special importance."

"It is through the process of reasoning that some people prefer to ignore questions concerning their birth, life on this planet and beyond. Others, choose to have faith in God and base their belief on the available holy scriptures. IT IS UP TO YOU to reflect and decide whether or not the scriptures on which you base your faith are free of doubt, and that you hold the right belief and as a result follow the true faith."

10

Mothers

"I'll always love my Momma, cause she's my favorite girl. You only get one, you only get one, yea." (<u>Intruders</u>) Indeed my mother is my favorite girl. Without her, not only would I not be here, I would not have had children. Thousands of people whom I have effected and have affected over my life time would not have been influenced by me, nor I by them; thus altering many things in their lives as well as mine, and so on, and so on, and so on. Thanks Mom...

Being a mother has got to be the most thankless job in the world. Children put their mothers through so much, it is almost unbelievable and definitely unfair. A mother will do almost anything for her child, unconditionally. Most men owe their mothers so much money, they have lost track of the amount. A mother knows secrets about you, you do not even know she knows. Remember what I said about keeping a secret? Every mother risks her own life, just to give birth. Although one of my very close friends who is a Gynecologist is more qualified to elaborate on the subject of birth than I will ever be, no one but the mother should decide to risk her life to produce another.

I could go on and on about many aspects of being a mother from what I have observed over the years; however, I am concerned with addressing just a few specific points as it relates to a mother's son. A mother can raise her child, a mother can raise a boy, and a mother can raise her son. The one thing she cannot do is raise a man.

Let us get serious about this matter, and allow me to open your mind to some cold hard facts. When a young man's penis gets erect and he does not understand why his body is acting that way, what do you say? Can a mother really explain how to get the erection back down, and deal with all the hundreds of questions that follow? If you do not know what I am talking about (unless you are a maturing young boy) you will never understand. What about show and tell? Boys naturally observe older men because they are curious to find out what is in store for them when they reach manhood.

How do you know the difference between a small penis and a large penis? All young men are constantly growing and want to know how long it will take for their penis to get to a size where they can feel proud; moreover, not be embarrassed. That is where fathers come in. It is a man thing. Like father, like son. Not only can a father answer these questions for his son, he can do it with such directness and tact, that the son will still feel comfortable asking questions. A mother just cannot do it. When I was a camp counselor, I used to over hear the young men talk about all sorts of growing pains. If no one gives them a decent answer, they will make up answers—usually wrong. How many mothers you know will have their 14 year old son naked in front of them while they are also naked in a locker–room; perhaps after finishing up a game of basketball, and explain the various parts of his body to him?

Then there is the sexual growth. Although men and women both enjoy sex, they approach it totally differently; especially at the teenager stage. The average penis starts practicing its erection involuntarily just after birth, to the best of my knowledge. No mother knows how that feels, unless she is a hermaphrodite. For what purpose does a penis get erect? Other than to embarrass you when you stand up sometimes, it is for sexual intercourse. If a young man's penis practices this routine of getting erect several times a day and in his sleep everyday for his entire life, he is going to want to know why. After he finds out why, he is going to want to find out how it works. It is that simple. If you owned an interesting tool all your life and finally found out what it was used for, wouldn't you want to test it out?

A father can not only explain the phenomenon of an erection, he can give personal examples to help a son feel that he is not suffering an isolated growth deficiency or efficiency. All men go through it. Depending on the age of a young man when he starts to ask questions, it might also be a good time to discuss sex, safe sex and no sex. A mother will say do not have sex until you are older, grown or some other type of excuse to get them to wait. A father will reflect on his youth and try to figure out how to prevent his son from having sex as young as he did, knowing the urge and desires are all there.

I remember a young man whom I ended up being a role model/ mentor for. He and I used to discuss all sorts of things. Most of the time it was the kind of conversations that his mother would not or could not talk about. As he got to be about 13 or 14 years of age, he started developing interest in girls. I would probe every now and then about him holding hands, kissing with the mouth open or closed and if he was having sex. Because of our father to son or big brother type trust and relationship, he would always be honest with me; after coaching it out of him sometimes, but he told me the truth. No he was not having sex.

One Christmas he and his mother invited my family, including my mother, over for dinner. He was still about 13 or 14 years of age. We all exchanged gifts and the one gift that caused the most excitement was the gift he received from his grandmother, who was also present at the dinner. His grandmother gave him a box of penis protectors. (Condoms) His mother almost had a heart attack. She snatched the box out of his hand and became hysterical. His mother was so upset at her mother for giving her son such a gift, they had to separate from each other for a few minutes. My mother and I just sort of looked at each other and smiled. It was a sight to see. Because of the emotions bubbling over, I decided to wait for another day to explain to the young man all about his grandmother's thoughtful gift, and why his mother got emotional. His mother was scared, as many mothers are, when they realize their son is becoming a man.

Now, on the flip side of the coin, I cannot really explain all that goes through a mother's head during that time. Perhaps some mothers have had bad experiences with sex when they were young girls and do not want their sons to do the same to someone else. Perhaps it was a painful or unpleasant experience. Perhaps they were raped. Perhaps they just know the way girls think and what they talk about, and do not want their sons to be the talk of the town. I do not know the reasons, because I am not a woman. Just as I am not qualified to teach and show my daughter how to deal with her first and subsequent menstrual cycles, due to my lack of experience, there are similar factors with a mother and her son.

While understanding the penis and the sexual curiosity of a boy is difficult, so is handling his masculinity. I have learned from experience and observation that a mother cannot control a 16 year old son, unless he wants to be controlled. If he does not want to be controlled, the mother will lose. A boy becomes a man by nature's definition some-where around age 15. His strength is developing so rapidly that even he does not know what his true capabilities are. One thing is for certain, he is closer to being a man than he is a boy.

This is the stage that has caused our nation to have the problems it has. This is the stage that only a father can handle. The guns, the drugs, the drop–outs, the teenage pregnancies, the violence, the crimes, the murders, the problems, the problems on top of problems are out of control at this stage. Mothers have no control, the cities have no con-trol, the states have no control, the government has no control. This is where the mother watches all her work and effort go down the drain. This is where a mother searches her mind endlessly to see where she went wrong. This is where she is forced to make the most difficult deci-sion of her life—the decision of disowning her son. Putting him out. Sometimes even having him arrested. This is where she becomes numb.

For this reason alone, I cannot see why young unmarried teenage girls feel that having a baby at a young age will make them feel grown. When she turns thirty, she might be living the worse nightmare of her life. Babies having babies is like playing Russian roulette, if your num-ber pops up, your life is over.

Why? After all a mother has done for her son, why? It is simple. The father did not do his job. The father is the only one who can control the son at this stage. Look around at how well all of our glorious insti-tutions are doing. They are all failing at their mission statement, while pointing the finger at the families and communities. A father is the only one who can solve the crisis we are having. As a father, I have solved the problems of a son for many mothers. Some temporary and some permanently. I had to alter their thinking process so that their mothers could have some degree of control. I did not necessarily use force, I used affection. We need all fathers to step in and do the same.

When I say fathers, I am not necessary talking about a man living in the same house with the mother and son. Sometimes this cannot always be the case. I have a friend who has been married twice and has three children between the two wives. He has since divorced and is now looking for a third wife. Although he is not living with his children, he does anything and everything he can for them. He loves his children more than he loves himself.

He has just given his first wife $20,000 towards buying a house and after practically purchasing it for her, she is now asking for another $10,000 to go into the house. I asked him why did he buy the house for her? He said because he wanted his children to live in a better neighborhood with less negative influences. He has told me many sad stories about this former wife. I had to ask him why did he marry her if she had so many problems? He said because she was pregnant with his child and he wanted to do the right thing. I told him that is one of the reasons why divorce rates are so high now.

Son, there are women out there who will get pregnant purposely to snare a good man. What most people fail to realize is that marriage is supposed to be permanent. It is supposed to be two sided, not one sided. It is supposed to be for the rest of your life—for better or for worse, until death do you part. Do not marry because it seems like the right thing to do. You will only hurt the mother and the child in the long run.

While working as a public housing manager at the Philadelphia Housing Authority, I had the opportunity to witness first hand, hundreds of single parent mothers trying to raise their sons. I have seen parents who really wanted to help their sons, but were helpless to the situation. The sons would come and go as they pleased. Some would disrespect their mothers in their face. They would not only take their mother's money, they would sell off some of their mother's possessions. I have seen seven year old sons ignore, curse at and sometimes even strike their mother. Yes I taught them a quick lesson on manhood when it happened in my presence, however, the behavior was ingrained.

I have had to contact various agencies to investigate child neglect of some of my tenants. On one occasion, the agency had to take the children from the mother because of the documented repeat infractions. The mother just left her children in the house while she went out to do her own thing such as drugs and other enterprising activities. The children who grow up in these sort of environments are no different than a child who grows up in a middle class environment with two parent families. They will imitate what they see and hear. They want to be accepted by the dominating social structure of their environment. Good, bad or indifferent, you are a product of your environment.

The young men on the corner selling drugs learned it from other young men on the corner selling drugs, not their mother. Most females are no match physically for men their age. Therefore, since only the strong survive, young men dominate the drug trade and territories. Since the only one who can really challenge the young men and change their behavior is another man, in most cases, a mother is helpless. Go to any housing development at night and just watch what goes on and who is doing it. Even if the women are selling themselves, it is the man who is running the show. If more fathers would take responsibility of their responsibilities, then these problems would not be as great as they have become.

When contemplating responsibility of a child out of wedlock, always try to keep the child's interest at heart. As a matter of fact, the child's interest should come before yours. It would be wiser to either take full custody of the child if it is a boy, or have equal custody. The main thing is to own up to your responsibility and help raise your child. I could go on a tangent about responsible sex; however, that will not solve the problem after the fact. The bottom line is that both the mother and father have to be mature about bringing a new life into the world and do what is best for the child. The child will be happier, the parents will be happier and there will be less stress overall.

Speaking of less stress, most mothers whose son joins the military and come back home, feel so proud of their son because of the change.

The change seems drastic because the last time she saw him he was what she was used to seeing; an unattended son. The next time she sees him he is very different. What she is looking at that is so different—that is so rewarding, is a man. She is looking at her son as a man, in most cases for the first time. A sharp, clean cut, mannerable, grown-up man. He is not only a man to be proud of, but also one to be respected.

The Military Training Instructor or Drill Sergeant is their father for the entire time of the training process. He sleeps, eats, walks, runs, works, trains, fights, cries, hurts, bleeds and even dies with them. He does not do it just because it is his job. He does it out of love. The love of his country, the love of his profession and the love of his fellow man. After he has made a boy into a man, he then passes him onto another fatherly figure who helps to continue his development process. I know there are female MTI's who have done outstanding jobs training their trainees, and I commend them for their efforts. However, if you were to ask a soldier what went through his mind when she spoke to him you might be surprised at the answer. The level of respect is not the same for a non–fatherly figure.

Turning boys to men is one of the reasons I became an Air Force Recruiter. In spite of all the attacks I took because of a few bad apples in the recruiting service, I was proud to be in the position to transform boys into men. I was the door. Through me, passed many boys who became men. I did not just put them in the Air Force. That would have limited me. I put them in the Army, Navy, Marines, Coast Guard, National Guards, Active Duty and Reserve. Although my first priority was putting them in the Air Force, those who did not qualify still needed help. So I helped them. Besides, it is a good feeling to help young men who are searching for direction. It is a feeling I wish I could share with everyone. It is the kind of feeling that sends goose pimples up your back, and tears down your face. God may have created us and women may have given birth to us, but men have made men. That is my job. The job of a father, not a mother.

I commend the Boot Camp theory and whom ever was instrumental in finally bringing a good idea to reality. The structure will need to be constantly improved with focus and a sense of direction for those it is intended to reform. It is a sensitive project, one which I hope this government takes seriously. Given the wrong decisions made on its behalf, it could also become a failure. I challenge that institution to transform boys to men. I challenge that institution to educate those men at the college level so that they will be equipped with the real ammunition to fight in this world. I also challenge the Boot Camp institution to act as a placement service to give the newly reformed and transformed young men jobs, housing and dignity when they are released; rather than just releasing them back to whence they came.

In the chapter on money and education, I talk about the psychology of what it does to a young man and to some degree, how to gain control. However, in this society, sometimes a person has lost the battle before even beginning due to their social status or some other circumstance. Many young men who have a record are basically good young men. Unfortunately, they were at the wrong place at the wrong time with no representation to assist them. As a result, they are sucked into the system. Now they are permanently marked.

How do you permanently remove that mark so that you can compete equally and fairly in this world? To rehabilitate a person is one thing. To train, educate and develop them is a responsibility. If the mother was not able to do it, then who can? The men that are rehabilitating them. It should be a comprehensive philosophy to strengthen our young men. That way, when he becomes an old man, he will not only be more productive; he will be able to pass on the knowledge he has acquired from a positive stand point.

As a boy grows older, his most inner desires and fears are that of becoming a man. He wants so much to be respected as a man. He knows it takes time, but he just does not want to wait. Before a young man gets to the point where a mother cannot handle him, a mother needs to find a man. Not for herself, but for her son. A man who is willing to provide guidance and help with the difficult task of making a man. A mother just does not have the experience.

I remember being told by several men whom I have challenged when I was a boy: "Reggie, I have been your age but you have never been mine." "I have been a boy but you have yet to become a man." My mother has and still does, remind me that I have never been her age. However she has never told me once, that she was a man.

Always love your mother, you only get one.

11

Health and Fitness

I feel that it is very important for me to mention something on the subject of health and fitness. Over the years I have managed to maintain my body in pretty good shape and health. In the beginning when I was a teenager, it was to look good for the girls. Having a sculptured body had many advantages. After marrying an extremely attractive young lady, having a muscular body kept the so called dogs away. People would size me up and not bother me or my wife because of my physical appearance. Now that I am older and have been married for over fourteen years, staying in shape is more for my personal health than those earlier reasons. Do not get me wrong, had it not been for those earlier reasons, I may be fighting an up hill battle, as many are now who are my age. So the ego paid off.

You need to keep your body running at its optimum level as much as you can. The body is one of the most complex one of a kind masterpieces on earth, therefore, it must be maintained if you want to keep it. Because your body has 70,000 miles of blood vessels and the heart has to pump blood through this labyrinth and back again once every minute, common sense should tell you that whatever you put into your veins gets pumped through your body. That is why drugs are so dangerous. All that stuff goes through your heart, as does alcohol–which many people thought only went to the brain. In one year the average human heart circulates from 770,000 to 1.6 million gallons of blood through the body, enough fluid to fill 200 tank cars, each with a capacity of 8,000 gallons. Therefore, since your heart is one of the most vital organs in your body, you need to be careful about what comes in contact with it.

Just as maintaining your heart is important, you must equally be concerned about your lungs. If they stop working, so do you. The human body cannot survive for more than a few minutes in an environment that lacks oxygen. Consequently, God has designed your lungs to operate without you having to think about it. They perform their function automatically, non stop every day for your entire life. Although many people are beginning to become aware of how important it is to take care of their heart, they are not equally educated and concerned about their lungs.

Oxygen is required for the normal functioning of all living body cells. This vital gas reaches the body cells via the bloodstream; each red blood cell transports oxygen molecules to the body tissues. Just as what you ingest goes through the heart, the same applies to what you breath. Whatever you breath goes through your entire body by way of the bloodstream. That is why air pollution and smoking are two of the most hazardous items in our atmosphere, however, they are controllable.

Most advanced martial arts practitioners are familiar with how important proper breathing is. As I said, breathing occurs automatically. However the parts that are not automatic are the other attributes which can also be obtained by breathing. There is a theory surrounding a word called, "Ki." The literal translation of Ki is air. However, Ki is much more an elemental force (life energy). Ki power makes change and influences all things, including non–living things. Many people refer to Ki power as energy, a vital force, nervous energy, or psychic energy. It takes practice, dedication and concentration; but once mastered, you will have unlocked one of the many mysteries of the world. Bruce Lee mastered the ability to knock a man down with a one inch punch. You can best believe he had full control of his Ki when he delivered his punch. Although you may never need to use a one inch punch, you will need to use the benefits of Ki. Now that you have been shown the path of Ki, it is up to you whether you take the journey.

Although your involuntary operational organs are extremely vital to your very existence, you have many other parts of your body which need to be maintained also. Your bones, your muscles and your skin are all items which have a direct effect on you. For instance, did you know that a simple, moderately severe sunburn damages the blood vessels to such an extent that it takes four to fifteen months for them to return to their normal condition? Did you also know that eighteen ounces of an average cola drink contains as much caffeine as a cup of coffee? Talk about drugs... Learn about what you put into and onto your body. Ignorance can be harmful.

Son, never, never, never allow yourself to become overweight. Most overweight children remain overweight as adults. Some did not do anything to control their weight at a younger age and as they grew older it became too difficult to deal with. A few are just happy and comfortable being large and would not change it for anything. Nevertheless, there are too many overweight people in this world. Because of fast foods and other conveniences, we are always eating and nibbling; in many cases once an hour. The problem is these same people are not exercising to get rid of the calories.

Excess weight is the result of the imbalance between caloric intake as food and caloric expenditure as energy, either in maintaining the basic metabolic processes necessary to sustain life, or in performing physical activity. Calories not spent in either of these ways become converted to fat and accumulate in the body as fat, or <u>adipose tissue</u>. There are some overweight people who have slow metabolism and for the most part are going to always be overweight. Perhaps their main concern is not to become obese. For those types of people it is more or less a medical condition they have to live with. For the rest of the world, the problem lies somewhere in their excuses.

Son, you must try to always stay in shape. The heart that pumps blood through a 400 pound overweight man is the same size as the one in a 200 pound healthy man. You would not use a car engine to run an eighteen wheeler tractor trailer would you? It is the same concept. Do not become that tractor trailer, you only have a car size heart. You do not have to be Mr. Fitness either, just be consistent. Try to exercise at least three times a week for 15—30 minutes. It will strengthen your bones, relieve depression, slow the aging process and ease stress and anxiety. Regular exercise will also improve your cholesterol profile, enhance your self image and improve the quality of your sleep. For the long term consideration, exercise can also reduce your risk of chronic diseases, improve your mental capacity and lower your risk of getting certain cancers. Do not wait until it is over due.

There is a very important piece of information you should know. It is so important that if I do not tell you, you might find out the hard way. It is inevitable, it is a sad fact, and it is a culprit that most people are fighting every day. When you turn "30 years of age", your body will turn against you. If you continue to eat the same amount of foods as you did at 20 years of age, when you turn 30, you will get fat. If you do not have a regular exercise routine in place, you will get fat. If you do not watch your caloric intake, you will get fat. If you do not believe what I am telling you, you will get fat. Do not let what has happened to the many disbeliever's happen to you. Most of them are still in the denial stage. Although it can happen anywhere between age 20 and 30, let age 27 be the warning stage and begin to prepare for the body transformation. You can believe me or not, but it will happen.

Presently I train about three times a week in Tang Soo Do martial arts. Not only is it healthy for me, it helps in other obvious areas also. Occasionally I will play tennis, basketball, football, table tennis or racquet ball to add diversity to my exercise routines. Hiking, skating, swimming, running and walking are also activities I enjoy to break the monotony. When my wife and I bought our first house, we stayed very active with home improvements. Carpentry, landscaping, masonry work, roofing, plumbing, painting and other home improvement projects kept us in shape. The main thing is to be conscious of your body and its needs. If you do not keep it running at optimum level, when you really need it, it will not perform.

Speaking of perform, I would like to shift to an area that is near and dear to the heart of most young men as well as older men. Let us talk about sports. Sports is viewed in many ways by many people. It has made millionaires and has sent others into the poor house. It has brought many people together and has separated marriages. It has given to some, incredible abilities and strength and has crippled others for life. Sports has caused all sorts of fights and battles, and it has calmed the fiercest crowds. For some, sports is everything, while for others it is nothing. As you travel through life, you too will find your rightful place in the world of sports.

From the time a child is born they are being introduced to sports. The very nature of play stimulates the muscles in preparation for future usage. Once a child is able to walk, he/she is introduced to other types of play to stimulate running. I am sure that world class runner and champion Carl Lewis had many running stimulus activities when he was a child. By the time a child reaches age three or four, he begins to develop specific interests based on his environment. It may be cold, warm, coastal, mountainous, urban, suburban, heavily populate, dense, agricultural, industrial, or technological, whatever the type, he will be influenced by his environment.

These influences will transcend into his school age years. This is where he begins to specialize in various sports. Whether it is basketball, baseball, football, hockey, tennis, swimming, gymnastics, karate, judo, boxing, wrestling, track and field, soccer or any other type of sport, the foundation of most particular sports is usually built during the school age years. With this foundation, many have gone on to establish professional careers in sports, while others were just content at achieving their short term goals. Sports has been for many people, a vehicle to achieve a means to an end.

Although for some, sports has given them a future, for others it has not. For every one success story in sports, there are a thousand wanabees. Keeping in mind that there are only 24 hours in a day, too many people waste their days just watching sports. Do not get me wrong, watching sports is good entertainment. I love watching sports when I have the time, especially the Superbowl, the Play–Offs, the Championships, the World Series, the Stanley Cup and other end of season games. The problem comes when that is all a person does. There are men with families and responsibilities who will neglect their responsibilities to watch sports for hours on end. They live for the game. They even know the stats of the teams and players better than some of the news casters. Unfortunately they are allowing sports to run their lives.

Watching sports on television for some is just plain old fun. They are seasonal with it, so the family understands and allows them their time. For others it is an addiction. They are living someone else's dream and success. I have seen fights break out over all sorts of stuff in the name of sports. If you say something wrong about someone's favorite player, they will fight in defense of that player. If you downgrade or belittle someone's team, that could start a riot. It is crazy how emotional people can get over sports. The part that really gets me is that none of the guys are getting paid to be spectators. As a matter of fact, they are the ones contributing to the players' salary, yet in most cases the players are not even aware of the individuals.

There is also the element of gambling, betting, suckering or whatever you want to call it. Big money is made and lost every day from all sorts of sports. People are betting now on who the MVP will be at the end of the season. Many people have various football pools and other group participation gambling activities. For some, it is how they earn a living. All they do is bet on sports.

For a while, I to used to bet on sports pretty often. After a while I learned my lesson. Since I never won, I could only count my losses. My losses added up to a healthy sum over a period of time. I then resorted to gambling on billiards only. Because I was pretty proficient at the game, and it was basically a one on one sport, the odds were more in my favor than betting on someone else. At least this way I had more control of the game.

Since those days, I have even given up betting on billiards. Don't get me wrong, I have won my fair share in billiards. I used to earn spending money for both me and my brother by hustling the pool table. It is just that I have become more practical with my money. Nevertheless, every once in a while I do come across someone whose mouth is bigger than his game. When that happens, the thrill of shutting them up is the challenge I accept. The money is usually their idea.

If you really want to learn something about gambling, look into the loser's eyes as he hands over his money to a smiling winner. Not only will you learn something, you might feel something as well. As long as there are sports, there are always going to be people betting on the game. I think the Romans had a lot to do with it. Just remember, at the end of the game there will be a loser and a winner. I hope you are a winner.

Sports is fun, but like watching sports on television, it can be addictive. Should you have a desire to pursue a career in sports I recommend you at least research the sport as much as you can. Find out everything about the sport. Study its history from its first conceptualization up to its present day changes. Talk to players and participants of the sport about their attitudes and personal feelings towards the sport. Some football players will tell you not to play football because of the permanent injuries you could sustain. Also talk to retired football players and other retired sports players. Get the real scoop—the truth. Always try to know as much about what you are getting into before you get into it. It helps you stay in it.

I would also like to point out that it is a very good idea to master as many activities as your ability allows while you are young. As you get older you will not have the time to learn too many new sports, not too mention your body may not be as cooperative either. Therefore, if you have mastered an activity at a young age, it will be part of your repertoire when you get older. It will also give you a wide range of activities to choose from, depending on your time and resources. So do not just learn one thing, learn them all. Besides, you will not only have fun doing it, you will be contributing to a healthy body.

I hope this chapter has helped you to understand a little more about health and fitness. I hope it also inspired you to learn more about your body and how to maintain it. Whether you become a professional sports athlete or not, I encourage you to partake in some sort of physical activities regularly for your entire life. Your heart and the rest of your body will be very thankful if you maintain a regular routine in some sort of physical activity. Medically, emotionally, spiritually, and of course physically, it is necessary to stay active. It also helps if you eat the right foods. After you reach thirty, you to will be thankful.

Good luck in maintaining the only body you have. Remember, there are no trade–ins, you have the original.

NOTES

Use this section to write down a few notes about yourself as it relates to health and fitness or any subject for that matter. Your notes will give you something to reflect on the next time you read this book. Don't forget to date it and put your present age.

You might want to put down the types of sports you enjoy watching or playing. Do you have a favorite team, player or position? Perhaps you are an ice skater, rollerblader, or surfer. How many push–ups can you do? Crunches? Pull–ups? How far can you run? One mile, two, maybe five. What's your pulse rate? Are you sick all the time? Overweight? Can you swim two lengths of the pool? Do you lift weights? Jot down a few notes now…

12

Hygiene

Hygiene could be considered as a part of health and fitness; however, I felt it needed to be addressed separately due to its distinct significance in your daily routine. Daily hygienic practice is one of the most over looked routines by so many people. Far too many people will come home after school or work, change into their party or play cloths, slap on some cologne and go right back out without even washing their hands. Even worse, I have known people to go home dripping with sweat who have done the same thing. That is disgusting. Here is a rule of thumb. If you smell yourself, others have already been smelling you for a long time. Not only is it disgusting, it is offensive. It is almost as bad as smoking around nonsmokers. Being conscious of your hygiene takes effort, however, the effort you expend will reward you with big dividends.

Some of the things we are told to do is wash our hands before eating, wash our hands after using the toilet, wash our hands after playing, wash our hands after handling animals, wash our hands before handling a baby and many more reasons. All these practices are good because you do not want to get or transfer germs. In addition to the germs, you also do not want to contract unconquerable viruses, parasites, or worms. Each one of those can make your life unbearable. Parasites alone can cause you bad stomach problems, severe weight loss, weakness, and worst of all, several days of diarrhea which can lead to dehydration. You will live on that toilet seat for quite a while, just because you did not wash your hands.

While living in Saudi Arabia I have experienced what it was like to have parasites. It can be a nightmare. One of my friends missed work for two weeks and spent the first week in the hospital due to parasites. When it was all over he was about 25 pounds lighter. There were times when almost one fourth of the entire community where I lived had parasites. All because the cooks did not wash their hands. Because there were so many foreign nationalities from third world countries, diseases were everywhere. I know of people who contracted hepatitis from shaking hands. Maybe that is why some nationalities bow instead of shake hands. The main point I am trying to express is the importance of washing your hands. Microscopic germs and parasites can cause severe problems, so wash your hands regularly.

Speaking of washing, how often do you shower or bathe? Many people will answer once a day. My next question to them would be, at what part of the day do they shower or bathe? I know people who traditionally shower before going to bed, wake up, get dressed and think they are clean. Wrong answer. They think they are clean, but in reality they were sweating in their sleep, as well as shedding some of their dead skin. Another factor is that they are about to get dressed for a 12 to 16 hour day after sleeping for about 8 hours. I would hate to be around them near the end of the day. Twenty hours without a shower can make a person pretty ripe.

Son, I am going to give you the lowdown on cleaning your body so that you will always know. As strange as it may sound, most people are not taught the fundamentals on cleaning themselves, which leads to hygienic problems. I recommend taking a shower at least once a day—preferably two showers. And depending on what type of activities you are involved in, maybe even more.

Of course the best time to shower is in the morning before going out to greet the world. Additionally, it also helps you to wake up and feel fresh before getting dressed. I also recommend taking a shower before going to bed. A dirty body and clean sheets just does not go together. Besides, having a clean body will help you to sleep more comfortably. The other benefit of showering before going to bed occurs if you wake up late and you are in a rush. Should you have to forego a shower due to time, at least you will not be as dirty as you would have been had you not taken a shower the night before. Those are just the basic times. Of course if you plan to go out in the evening, after going all day without refreshing yourself, it is always wise to shower before going out again. This way, not only will you look clean, but you will be clean all over.

When taking a shower, you must pay special attention to the vital areas. By that I mean the areas that collect the most dirt. Unfortunately, some people just glance a bit of soap over their body and that is it. They think they are clean. Wrong answer. They are rinsed, but not clean. You need to scrub the vital areas, not just glance over them. Wherever the skin folds over to create a moist warm environment, you are bound to have sweat and bacterial growth. The bacteria is what creates the odors. These are what I call the vital areas. There are several others which I will also go over one by one so that there is no misunderstanding about whether you are clean or not.

After you get into the shower, rinse off all the surface dirt first. Once you have rinsed all the surface dirt off, begin to work on the vital areas. I recommend scrubbing those vital areas at least three times (that's scrub, rinse, scrub, rinse, scrub, rinse) with a good soaped up wash cloth or luff. If you have any specialized soil on your body like grease, paint, oil or other hardcore soil, start there. If you just had your hair cut, start there. Also starting from the top and working your way down is a good way to make sure you covered all areas.

One vital area that seems to always harbor dirt is the neck. If you have ring around the collar, then your neck needs to be scrubbed thoroughly. Do not just scrub the neck only, make sure you go all around and up and down to all the other parts that the neck attaches to. While you are there, clean your ears inside and out. Do not worry too much about the water getting into your ears, gravity or a good Q–tip swab will take care of that after you get out of the shower.

Now that you have begun your cleansing, it is time to tame those underarms. Scrub–a–dub–dub... Do not forget to rinse your wash cloth and reload with soap to insure you have accomplished your task. The underarm needs to be scrubbed thoroughly. While you are in the area, extend your range for any stray bacterial critters. Remember you are dealing with a vital area and vital areas require special attention. Try using a white wash cloth every now and then to see how well you are cleaning yourself.

One overlooked area is the back. Your back sweats just like any other part of your body. Although it is hard to reach, you need to do your best. Generally it is not washed as often as it should be, so when you do wash it make sure you are making up for all the times you did not. A back scrubbing brush or Luff can assist you with this task. If you are out of shape or not too flexible, this will seem more like a painful challenge than a soothing shower.

Now let us talk dirty. Son, this next area has all the characteristics of a vital area. It is warm, moist, the skin folds over other skin and it produces sweat. You must pay special attention to cleaning your penis and the areas around it. You need to stretch the skin while washing it thoroughly. The skin underneath the penis where it attaches to the scrotum is where you will also find lots of buildup. While you are in that area, make sure you wash your scrotum well. As with the other vital areas, I recommend using a white wash cloth to truly learn how well you are washing yourself. The intensity of the dirt will reveal itself to you on the wash cloth and you will learn how well you are cleaning yourself.

Another way to determine if you washed your genital area well enough is whether or not you are constantly scratching yourself. There are a lot of guys who perpetrate looking cool by grabbing themselves between the legs or scratching themselves all the time. The truth of the matter is, they either never properly washed themselves, or they need to wash again. The bacteria is a living organism that is causing the itching sensation, not too mention an odor.

As I mentioned earlier, bacteria is what causes the odor. If you just glance over your body with soap and water, you might not be killing all the bacteria. Have you ever smelled someone with a foul odor, although they recently took a shower? Generally it is because they do not know how to wash and they only took care of the surface dirt instead of getting rid of the bacteria. When washing the vital areas, it is important to remember that you are not just washing off dirt, you are killing bacteria as well.

Son, there was a comedian who had a recording title which specifically dealt with washing. His name was Redd Foxx. He shared with the world a hygienic phrase that I have not forgotten. Because of its appropriateness, I would like to share it with you. He said, "You've got to wash your ass." "Not just your whole ass, but your ass hole." He later explained in more explicit terms, why. However, for the integrity of this book, I will just tell you the recording is very funny. Nevertheless, the buttocks is a vital area which needs complete attention. Your buttocks possess all the characteristics of a vital area. It is warm, moist, the skin folds over other skin and it produces sweat, as well as other matter. Please take heed to what the late Redd Foxx has so eloquently expressed.

The rest of the body, i.e., legs, feet, arms, etc., depends on what your activities are. Of course you need to wash your entire body, but you need to spend a little extra time on the vital areas. When it comes to your face, be careful not to mess your skin up with harsh soaps. I recommend using a facial bar or cleanser specifically for the face. If you do not have anything but regular soap, be gentle. While you are in the shower, do not forget to flush out your nose. If you are engaged in sports, or other physical activities, I recommend being clean before engaging in the activities and definitely shower after the activity.

Once you have cleaned your body, use a good deodorant under your arms. Some deodorants may be more compatible with your body chemicals than others, so try several until you find a few that work well and smell nice. You also need to moisturize your skin. Keeping healthy skin not only looks good, it feels good too. If you have problems with foot odor, you should use a good foot deodorant to control athlete's feet. Although not everyone has this problem, for those that do, it can be quite serious. The practice of splashing or spraying on cologne is generally done after showering. When using cologne, make sure it is compatible with your skin and natural body odor. What smells good on one person may not smell the same on another. The other caution I would like to warn you against is not to over do it. Too much cologne is just as offensive as a person who needs to wash more often. If you are not sure about how much to use, just ask someone with good judgment to give you their opinion.

Just as washing your body regularly is helpful to your health and others, so is cleaning your mouth. A dentist can tell you how many germs are in the mouth, I am here to tell you a few things on keeping most of them away, as opposed to keeping people away. Most people brush at least once a day—which is nice. I recommend brushing about three to five times a day. If you talk a lot, or if talking is how you earn a living, then your mouth needs to be cleaned more often than someone who does not talk for a living. Not only should you brush, you need to floss.

Although most people tend to focus on the teeth, the bacteria is all over the mouth, not just the teeth. Because of this, you need to brush your tongue. Try rubbing your tongue up against the roof of your mouth and see if you feel a coating of bacteria. The critters almost always lingering in the back of your mouth which means you have to brush there also. If you're like most people, you will probably gag from this experience. It's ok. Gagging is ok. Don't over do the brushing of your tongue in the rear of your mouth. Just get that film off. Then your mouth will really be clean.

Some people say you should floss once a day. I say floss as often as you need to. Depending on what you eat, a tooth pick just does not cut it. When you have something stuck between your teeth, there is nothing like the feeling of floss to rescue you from that irritating feeling. Speaking of eating, I also recommend you rinse your mouth out with water after eating. Do it for a week and watch all the stuff that comes out and you will be doing it for the rest of your life, especially after eating popcorn.

Speaking of floss, I have an idea which may or may not be patented yet. Instead of those flavored tooth picks the restaurants give you after a meal, they could give you a twenty inch length package of floss. Now that is a money maker. I do not have the time to research whether or not it is already patented. However, if it is not, it could be a money maker.

After cleaning your teeth, you need to clean your mouth. Many people think that just because they brush their teeth, their breath will not smell bad. Wrong answer. You cleaned your teeth, not your mouth and throat. You need to wash your mouth out with something that also fights bacteria and plaque. A good bacteria and plaque fighting mouthwash should do the trick.

After doing all that, and you still have bad breath, you should see a dentist. A dentist might have to clean your teeth and gums professionally. Most of the times a routine checkup (which generally does not hurt) will clear it up.

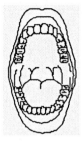 Regular oral hygiene will help to make the trip to the dentist painless. If you do not maintain good oral hygiene, you will allow those germ critters to cause you big problems. Consider the germs in your mouth like an army. Perhaps a few thousand microscopic critters preparing for an attack. As you eat, they eat. Just like you, these germs excrete waste products after eating. These waste products are bacterial acids which begin to cause tooth decay. Since these germs are like us, there are foods they like and foods they do not like. There are also foods they digest better than others. The easiest food for them to digest is sugar. The more sugar you eat, the more they eat. The more they eat, the more waste they excrete. The more waste they excrete, the faster your tooth may decay. So leaving the slightest food particles in your mouth, will literally be feeding an army.

The other reason you should brush and floss often is to get rid of the plaque. This monster, if left unattended, will get stronger by the hour. Once he reaches his full strength, only a dentist has the power to beat him. That sticky mucus type stuff you scrap off of your teeth is plaque. It generally begins its journey of growth after a meal, usually at the gum line. Once it has begun to mix with all the other moist stuff in your mouth, it becomes thicker, usually white. This is called materia alba. At this point, you must brush and floss or else it will be too late. If you do not get rid of it, it will become like epoxy cement. Once it sticks, it will become as hard as stone. This is tarter. Tarter can only be removed professionally. Tarter will also cause you to lose all of your teeth.

Oral hygiene is more important than most people realize. I remember while on a business trip in St. Louis, my gum was swollen around one tooth. I did not pay much attention to it because I felt it would go down eventually. After a few weeks, I started to feel a slight irritating feeling. One night I woke up at about 1:00 a.m. in pain. I had never experienced that type of pain in my life. It brought tears to my eyes. I ran to the mirror in the bathroom and looked into my mouth to see what it was. It was that swollen gum. Because I was in a hotel in another state, I did not know who to call. I put ice on it, I took aspirin, I even tried to pull the tooth out myself. I took a paper clip and stuck it down the side of the gum to see if I could get the pain out. Actually the paper clip some how relieved the pain long enough for the ice to go to work. I never did get to sleep that night.

At about 7:00 a.m. I was calling the dentist for an emergency appointment. He saw me right away. He said I had an abscessed tooth. He explained that it was because my oral hygiene was not adequate. Much to my dismay, he also told me he would not be able to drain the abscess for a couple of days. He did however prescribe lots of medicine for me. The pain killer was my main concern.

Not only did he tell me all about how I acquired the abscess and relieved my suffering, he explained what it was and why he had to wait a few days before draining it. He said the medicine was to help neutralize the abscess because the abscess was actually poison. Almost like a snake's venom, only not as bad. He said he did not want the poison to get into my blood stream from the work because if it got into the blood stream it would travel to my heart. If an abscess gets to your heart, it could be fatal. Talk about scared. Since then, I am now a believer in good oral hygiene.

Although good oral hygiene is very important, I would like to also talk about hair. If you allow your hair to grow long, you need to keep it cleaned, groomed and free of insects. In the seventies and earlier, many people sported Afros, and other types of styles with long hair. It was the fad then. It was also more difficult to manage than short hair. It took longer to wash and longer to comb. If bugs were to build a home in your hair, it might be some time before you realize it. If some sort of scalp disease were to begin to form in your hair, it too may take some time before you notice it. The answer is to keep it at a relatively short style. A shorter style is not only easier to manage, it also looks good.

As for having a beard, just like the scalp, the cleaning and grooming rules also apply here. You may need to be cautious of shaving bumps as you get older. Generally you will notice an itching sensation and bumps under your neck and around other areas where your hair is growing. This can cause your pores to clog, and in some cases, infection. Some say the problem is best handled by shaving with the grain, using a sharp blade, not an electric one. There are all sorts of stuff on the market that is suppose to stop, soothe, or relieve the problem. However, I recommend consulting someone specialized in this area before experimenting on your face. The one thing that seems to be universal in solving the problem is allowing the hair to grow for a while. Personally I prefer to be clean shaven. However, every once in a while I do let it grow. Usually on vacations.

Good grooming does not just stop at your hair, you also need to pay some attention to your nails. Not just your finger nails, but your toe nails as well. Keep them clean and cut. All sorts of nasty stuff hides underneath your finger nails. Even after washing your hands, there is still deposits of dirt left under your nails. If you really want to enjoy an experience, have them professionally cleaned and trimmed. You will find it very interesting. Besides, once you have your nails professionally done, you will have learned how to properly do it yourself.

These are just a few of what I consider very important hygienic concerns which you need to know about. As you can see, it is very important to pay attention to detail when it comes to your body. From head to toe, you need to be in good form. Not only will you smell good, but you will also look good and feel good too. Remember, what separates two people most profoundly is a different sense and degree of cleanliness.

13

Sex

If you think this chapter is going to be about pornography, you are wrong. If you think this chapter is going to get into the nuts and bolts about sex, you are close. What I am going to attempt to do is cross the line, which most parents have preferred to stay behind. Although I am nowhere near being as qualified as Dr. Ruth may be to talk about sex, I am a father and I have a responsibility to you as my son.

Most parents, teachers and friends are not doing such a good job at sex education. If they were, we would not have the severe problems we have today. Teenage pregnancy and venereal diseases between the 13 and 18 years of age group is outrageous. Although I will be the first to tell you not to have sex until you are older and more responsible, preferably after you are married, I am also realistic enough to understand that the urges are there.

Long ago when we were in the agricultural age, young people found out about sex through working on the farm. The animals had sex all the time and they would watch. They would also assist in birthing the animals. Sometimes they would even assist in cross breeding to increase their farm's commercial options. These practical experiences helped them to learn the truth about sex in many ways. Unfortunately in this day and age, the average curious youngster will not be able to get practical experience from a farm. Instead, they get the practical experience and knowledge from the television and friends.

Ninety nine percent of what you see on television is not what you call making love. Love is not made in the bed, it is in the heart. Sex has nothing to do with it. Love is an emotional feeling that you share with and for someone. Generally the people you love, you are not interested in having sex with. As a father, I have an unconditional love for you but I am not going to have sex with you to prove it. That is sick. Nevertheless, you hear people on the television say "let's make love", as if love were a tangible object.

Another media term is, "going to bed". When you go to bed, generally it means you are tired and want to go to sleep. And the term "sleep with me tonight" is another exploited slang by the media. Again, if you go to sleep, you cannot have sex. You are sleep! These words and phrases you hear on the television are all to help stimulate a fantasy in the people who are watching it. Many of those actors are married. It is their job to make you believe that what they are saying is true. At the end of the day, the actors go home to their wives and children just like everyone else. The difference is, they get paid for making you believe that what they said was true, when in actuality, it was all an act.

Just as the movie industry will fill your head with all sorts of make believe fantasies, so will your friends. For some reason, friends seem to know all the answers. They will tell you all sorts of lies and you will fall for them because you did not know better. They will tell you what sex means, what it is all about and how you should be trying to catch up to their experiences. They will even brag about not being a virgin and tease you because you are. They will try to pour the peer pressure on so thick, you will begin to start believing them. This is where you need to be in control of your own thoughts and begin to consider the consequences. Just like driving a car, going to college, buying a house, being promoted to a high level position, there will come a time when sex will happen for you. If it happens too soon, you could prevent all the other inevitable goodies from happening, just because you did not wait.

Growing up in the city allowed me to see many of my friends, lives cut short in their prime because they made a wrong decision. I knew some very attractive young ladies who quickly became less than choice because they got pregnant at 13 and 14 years of age. These same young ladies are now in their 30's trying to salvage what is left of their lives. Some never finished high school so they are going back to get their GED. Some are so hooked on governmental assistance, they do not have the courage or desire to better themselves. Some are even grand-mothers. Although a few have made it in spite of having a baby at a young age, they were not able to really grow. They were not able to go to college and grow in their profession to become established like they wanted to.

The young men are no different. They either spend the rest of their teenage years denying the child and fighting the family of the girl they had sex with, or they are running themselves ragged trying to help support their child. This also leads to their dreams and aspiration being curtailed because of their responsibilities.

Besides the possibility of having children, there are diseases out there just waiting for the chance to claim you as a victim. Each year more than 300,000 American teenagers become afflicted with some form of venereal disease. Some of the diseases are temporary and some are permanent, but they are all painful in one form or another. Your penis could have a burning sensation so bad, you will be afraid to urinate because of the pain. You could even go blind. Your skin could also begin to develop irritating sores which come back periodically, for the rest of your life. Your muscles could stop working. You could even die. All this because you listened to your friend who thought he knew everything. Is the risk worth it?

If one should decide to chance the risk, it would probably be because he used a condom. I have many friends who thought the same thing. Unfortunately, they are now suffering from what I call the after sex syndrome. In many cases condoms leak. Have you ever opened up a pack of balloons and begin blowing it up only to find out that the balloon was defective. Same concept. Not only do condoms leak from a defect, some will tear while you are having sex. Then there is sabotage. There are cruel people who purposely slit the condom inside the packages with a razor blade before it is even sold to the stores. All these scenarios spell disaster for the person who assumed he was protected.

There is a saying: when you have sex, you also are having sex with every partner the other person has had sex with. That can be scary. If you were to see all the partners you are also having sex with, you might not even want to kiss the girl.

I told you all this because your friends generally will not. They will, however, prove me right by ending up just like some of the scenarios I just mentioned. It is a sad fact, but true. Another fact is that girls who have intercourse early in life, particularly before the age of sixteen, are twice as likely to develop cancer of the cervix as those who do not begin having intercourse until they are in their twenties.

Sex in its most primitive form is strictly for reproduction. No other animal exploits the reproductive organs as man does. Reproduction goes hand in hand with survival of the fittest. Some animals reproduce thousands of babies at a time because only a portion will survive. Some animals reproduce monthly because they have a short life span. Some animals reproduce annually because man kills them off so fast.

Long ago even man reproduced differently. Having a large family was necessary for survival. Food was not purchased from the store, it was grown, found and hunted. This took lots of help which necessitated a large family. Everyone had a specific job in the family. The men were the providers and protectors for the family, while the women would tend to the house and raise the children. It was not uncommon for women to get pregnant at a young age because they were married.

Long ago, women married as young as age 12. In some countries they still do. As a new wife, one of her duties was to begin making a family in order survive. By age twenty she might have given birth to about five children. This was part of her contribution to the tribe. As the children grew older, they too would assume the roles of growing, finding and hunting food. Since there were no senior citizen homes, when a person became very old, they also relied on all their children to take care of them until they died.

As you can see, having sex at a young age now, versus then, has very different meanings and purposes. Nevertheless you are a young man with urges and your curiosity can sometimes be overwhelming. On that note, I will tell you this corny, but pertinent analogy. If a person were painting a beautiful masterpiece for you which took six months to complete, and you decided you could not wait the full six months and bought it after only two months; you would never know the true beauty of what you have. Not only that, all you possess now is an unfinished painting, rather than a thing of beauty.

Son, you have to make your own decisions for yourself. In making decisions concerning sex, please use proper judgment along with good morals. Sexual intercourse can be a beautiful experience. It is not only sharing an experience, it is sharing each other. It is a feeling which cannot be expressed verbally because for everyone it is different. The longer you practice abstinence and self discipline, the more beautiful it will be. Preserve yourself until you know it is right, not when you think it is right.

14

The Game

Is government politics, or is politics government? Some would argue that they both are one in the same, while others would concede that they are inseparable. Nevertheless, the one thing that is for certain is that both government and politics have a profound impact on your life, and to a large degree, how you are allowed to live it. This is why you must approach how you navigate through life as if you were trying to win a game.

Certainly you cannot play a game if you do not understand the rules. Once you have learned the rules, you can begin to play. Like most games, your desire is to win, or at least not to lose; so you generally play to win. Unfortunately, sometimes the rules change. This is where a true master of the game is separated from a novice. A true master of the game not only knows the rules, he knows how to use them in his favor and against you. A true master of the game is, in actuality, a master of the rules. He does not follow the rules that are spelled out as most good players do. He studies the rules as opposed to studying the game. Once he has mastered the art of studying the rules, then he is in the position to change them. A true master of the rules can change them in his favor and even have you agree with him. A true master is a thinker, not just a player.

In the game of life there are many players, but only a few masters; Similar to the way there are many have–nots, but only a few haves. In this chapter I am going to give you an insight into what I call "The Game." Others have termed it, the game of life. I am going to take what you have already seen, heard, tasted, smelled, or felt in your own life, and present it back to you differently. Since you are a player in this game, I would advise you to play to win. That means learn the rules and think.

PREAMBLE

We the people of the United States, in order to form a more perfect Union, establish justice, insure domestic tranquillity, provide for the common defense, promote the general welfare, and secure the blessings of liberty to ourselves and our posterity, do ordain and establish this Constitution for the United States of America.

The preamble is the introduction to the constitution. It states reason and purpose. The Constitution is as the late Dr. Martin Luther King Jr. used to call it, a social political document. This document of ours contains all the rules to the game. The problem is that most United States citizens do not understand the rules. As a matter of fact, many citizens have never even read the preamble. I highly recommend that you read the constitution. As a matter of fact, you need to read the entire document from beginning to end. Although you will not understand all that you read, you will learn a lot from its contents. I also recommend that you reacquaint yourself with the constitution least once every five years to allow your five year increment experiences to help you learn more than you did the last time you read it.

In learning the rules, you must also learn to analyze the information from the authors' original intent. This takes practice, diligence and experience; however, once you are able to comprehend your new abilities, a new world begins to open up to you. Once you are able to understand the origin of the information, then you can apply it to the present.

The preamble can be understood or misunderstood. Depending on who is reading it and for what reason they are reading it, thousands of meanings can be derived from it. Let us look at it from a struggling African American mans frame of reference and see what happens.

WE the people of the United States. Who? Who are the we in "We the people"? On the first Wednesday of March, 1789, which is when the Government under the constitution was declared in effect, blacks were still slaves, so who is the "WE" referring to? Blacks were not even considered citizens during those times. Therefore, given all present knowledge of past history, it would be a safe assumption that the "we" was not counting blacks as a part of the United States. If that is the case, then it is also safe to assume that this document was written with a European mentality. Like owning dogs, horses and cattle, blacks in 1789 were still considered as property. This mentality is the basis for the rules that we are (as United States citizens) obligated to follow.

In order to form a more perfect union. First of all, no person, place or thing is perfect. With the exception of God and God's creation, nothing is perfect. This leaves the question of how can any God fearing human being bring his cerebral process to the point of thinking he is perfect. The second fact that really makes me question what kind of thought process our so–called forefathers used, is that they wanted to form a more perfect union than the perfect union they allegedly already possessed.

Looking at the two phrases we have already used, (We the people of the Unites States, in order to form a more perfect union) you should by now be able to surface useful information from your own subconscious to enable you to begin to understand the rules of the game. As I stated earlier, thousands of meanings can be derived from it. I am only trying to help you understand how to learn and use the rules of the game, not interpret them all for you.

Establish justice. Just us? Who? What? Where? Why? When? Which? How? This is how you need to approach this phrase. We know the who part, however, what kind of justice were they trying to establish and for what reason? I guess establishing the justice was part of the plan to form the more perfect union. Since there are several types of justice, the "which" question is also very valid here. Poetic justice, communistic, democratic, racial, medieval, which? These are all valid questions that the rules should spell out clearly so that there is no room for interpretation. These are the types of questions that you must have the answers to in order to understand the rules.

How was the justice established? Did they kill everyone who did not agree so that the Constitution would be ratified? Did they bribe the ones who disagreed? Did they publicly lynch or burn the opposition as was customary to those who went against the establishment? Did they request the expertise of slaves so that blacks would also embrace this new document that has been the number one governing factor in the United States for over 200 years? If questions like these do not pop into your mind, then maybe your brain should be re–washed. For it is the answers to these questions which hold the key to your very mystery.

Insure domestic tranquility. Tranquility means quietness; a calm state; freedom from disturbance or agitation; the state or quality of being tranquil. Again the same basic questions apply. Who? What? Where? Why? When? Which? How? The "how" and "why" questions are where I think the most revealing information will be found. Another fact that stands out like a sore thumb is that the preamble specifically stated <u>domestic</u> tranquility as an important fact. If the oath of office for many politicians is to uphold and defend the Constitution of the United States, why are we trying to insure foreign tranquility while failing at insuring domestic tranquility?

Although I do understand the reasons for foreign policies, I would never pay everyone else's bills while the creditors are pounding on my door, ringing my phone and sending me overdue notices. How can I feed everyone else while my own children are starving? I must first clean up my own house before I can help clean someone else's. Not only is it constitutional, it is common sense; yet, we are failing in this category by leaps and bounds. Where is the tranquility? As a United States Citizen, we pay our public servants (Politicians) to insure that our rights are being upheld. Therefore, just like terminating any employee who continues to demonstrate lack of performance or non–compliance in the position or duties in which they are assigned, they too should be terminated. Nowhere in the Constitution does it say that the employee is to control their employer when incompetence has been established on the employees part. When the slaves (servants) demonstrated incompetence, lack of performance or non–compliance, they were publicly whipped until they changed, or were killed if they would not change. My–my–my how the table has turned.

Looking at this phrase as it relates to the state of our country, it should demonstrate to you how much we adhere to our constitution. It is a crime that we do not have domestic tranquility. Many people are in violation of that crime from the top down and are not being held accountable for their responsibilities.

<u>Provide for the common defense.</u> Why do we provide for the common defense? What is a common defense in the first place? If it is so common, then why is it so difficult to understand? Ask twenty people today, "What is a common defense?" I bet you will get twenty different answers. I served close to ten years active duty in the United

Stated Air Force and I am not even sure what a common defense is. I even raised my hand and took an oath. Yet, there are stated provisions in the Preamble to provide for a common defense in order to form a more perfect union. Perhaps it was meant to be confusing.

Given the information gathered so far, it seems that a lot is involved in forming a more perfect union. I am also starting to wonder when and if this more perfect union was ever achieved and how long it maintained its more perfect union status. After all, I am a United States Citizen and I am entitled to a more perfect union; especially if the United States Government is entitled to my money in the form of taxes—or is it? ("Taxes", that is another book)

In taking a serious look at the common defense, I would say that there are a lot of people failing at their job. There are far too many innocent people dying because their common defense is not being provided for. People are not just dying from natural causes any more, they are dying from gun shots, drugs, toxic waste, governmental special projects, low self esteem, poverty, neglect, starvation, homelessness and environmental non–protection. Why? Because we are not being defended properly. As the saying goes, "Never send a boy to do a man's job, he'll just come back a boy, whereas a man will come back with results." We need results!

Promote the general welfare. The condition of health, prosperity and happiness; well–being. This is what welfare is. Somewhere along the lines of interpretation, I think this was mis–interpreted. Our government has abused promoting the general welfare ever since the ratification of the Constitution. I guess, because no one stopped them. Nevertheless, it is important to continue to understand that most of the phrases in the preamble hinge upon forming a more perfect union, which is a mentality that should not be. Perhaps that is why it took so many years before we finally put on our U.S. currency, "In God We Trust." Apparently some of our Country's founding forefathers did not trust in God, or did they think they were equal to God?

And secure the blessings of liberty to ourselves and our poster-ity. At first glance the average reader will not really understand this phrase. In dissecting just the word liberty, you will learn that from that word alone, the Constitution of the United States was not written with the African American in mind at all. It did not apply to us. Therefore, the input, the contribution, the emotional state, philosophies, the genetic blueprint and the balance of the African mentality was deliberately omitted from the Constitution. On that note, one could contend that the Constitution was written with extreme bias and prejudice. Perhaps that is why it is so difficult to defend in this era. Perhaps that is why so many people have a blatant disregard for its values. Perhaps that is why Mike Tyson went to jail for rape while others did not. Maybe that is why African Americans appear to be treated unjustly and unequally when it comes to the judicial system. They had no input in its construction.

The word liberty means freedom or release from slavery, imprisonment, captivity, or any other form of arbitrary control. When a person's Constitutional rights are found to be violated, generally some sort of acceptable restitution is made. How can the United States Government make an acceptable restitution to an entire nation of people whose Constitutional rights were and continue to be so freely, openly and blatantly violated? Impossible? No, it is not impossible. It may be unlikely, but not impossible. If we can provide billions of dollars to other countries, then we can provide restitution to those United States citizens whose ancestral generations have been Constitutionally violated.

Not only was the Constitution designed to secure the blessings of liberty to themselves, but also their posterity. Posterity means all of a person's descendants. To argue the fact that slavery happened long ago and there is nothing that we can do to change what happened in the past, is a very politically correct statement. To say that we cannot do anything because of the past, is a lie. We are the ancestors of victimized, abused, molested, violated, raped, manipulated, hindered, impaired, exploited, brutalized, demoralized and plagiarized United States citizens. Where is the posterity of that liberty? Why is there such a large difference between the haves and the have–nots? Why has there never been a black president? Look at the percentage of whites versus the percentage of blacks in the United States and statistically speaking, based on the percentage and not racism, there should have been at least fifteen presidents and vice–presidents of color. Where does the liberty and posterity truly "lie?" It is obvious.

Do ordain and establish this constitution for the United States of America. To decree, to order, to establish and to enact, is what ordain means. Blacks could not even vote then, let alone read, so who ordained and established it, and for whom?

Indeed it would be a remarkable accomplishment to truly uphold the Constitution of the Unites States and its values. Although it is clear that the Constitution was designed, drafted and ratified, without the thought of blacks being anything other than property, let alone free United States citizens; the fact of the matter is, African Americans are United States citizens and are entitled to the identical rights, benefits and privileges that our Constitution affords to the posterity of its draft-ers.

Perhaps that is why there are groups advocating white supremacy. They know that once the African American is able to interpret the Constitution correctly, an enlightening evolution will occur. This evo-lution will decrease the white power, money and status. As I stated ear-lier, you have to learn the rules of the game. The Constitution of the United states is the rules of the game of being a United States citizen. Out of the thousands of words that make up the Constitution, I only used 51 to show you that there is more to the rules then meets the eye.

As mentioned earlier, I chose to look at the Preamble from a strug-gling African American man's frame of reference to see what happens. It can be looked at from a woman's point of view, a child's point of view, a foreigners frame of reference, etc. In doing so, I would like to point out that I do not hold the present government responsible for our past. I do, however, hold it responsible for upholding the constitution and performing in its elected and appointed positions as outlined in the Constitution. That's accountability.

In contrast to our constitution, if you were to travel and live in another country, you would find a different set of rules to the same game. For instance, you can steal something in the United States, go to jail and be back out on the streets that same day, only to repeat the crime again. You may even repeat this process of going in and out of jail as a way of life. In Saudi Arabia, however, you could have your right hand chopped off for theft. Not only could you have your hand chopped off, you could have your head chopped off for committing a crime.

Different values, different morals and different cultures establish different ways of governing themselves. Whether you travel to Africa, Europe, Asia or the Middle East, you will encounter a different set of rules to the game. If you know the rules, you can play the game. If you master the rules, you can win. Keeping in mind, as stated in the chapter on communication, you should also learn the languages of the different countries you may travel to. That is one of the first rules of the game. If you cannot understand what is being said, you might as well not even try to play.

I have been to several countries where I witnessed and heard about acts, incidents and situations which might be considered illegal in the United States. I have seen women topless in public at an outdoor cafe' while eating lunch. I have watched hash and marijuana being smoked in public places openly and freely because it was legal in that country. I have witnessed prostitutes working their guild in public just like any other working person. They were even registered with the state as prostitutes because it was an occupation. I have been passed by cars on the highway doing well over 100 mph. As a matter of fact, if I were to have been hit in the rear, it would have been my fault for not moving over in time for the other car to pass me. I have seen the results from a police officer punching a man in the nose to collect blood for a blood/alcohol test because the man refused to cooperate. I have been to weddings where it is customary to shoot off guns every time new guests arrive. All these experiences and more might be considered unconstitutional or against the law in the United States; however, in other countries it is considered normal and within the law.

As with the United States Constitution, there are rules to everything you will encounter. The difference between the person who gets an "A" in school and the person who gets a "B" or "C" is not always because of how smart he is or is not. In many cases it is because one understood the rules to the game better than the other.

At my first college I graduated at the associates level with a 2.32 GPA. At another college, I graduated at the baccalaureates level with a 3.69 GPA. Although I was the same person, the major difference in my GPA increase came from a better understanding of the game. Yes I did learn more and yes I did study smarter, but it was all attributed to my having a deeper understanding of the game of education and its rules. Had I known and understood those rules as a young child, I might be a lot farther in my academic achievement. Hopefully you will not commit the same errors I have committed educationally.

Additionally, in all working environments there are obvious rules to the game and not so obvious rules to the game. It is the person who understands these rules that generally surpasses everyone else. I have heard all sorts of name calling of these types of people, (loners, brown nosers, workaholics, fast burners, etc.) but seldom have I heard them called achievers. Yet, that is what most of them are, "achievers." They want to better their condition in life. They want to provide more for their families. They want to achieve what their abilities say they are capable of achieving.

All work and no play makes Reggie a dull boy. Generally, play is where you begin to learn the games and develop your competitiveness. If you are playing sports, you have to know the rules or you will lose. In video games you have to know how to operate the controls, score points and not lose your man. There are magazines published specifically for teaching one how to win at the video games. Once you have mastered the video games, the knowledge learned can be transferred into real life situations. Your decision making process and strategic approaches to wining the video game are very similar to wining other games. All you have to do is master the rules.

No matter where you are, what you do, or who you are, you will have to learn the rules to many of life's games if you want to succeed. It takes more than just a desire to learn and understand these rules, but a desire is where you begin. Over time, hopefully you will learn to master these rules. Although the true rules and meanings to these rules may be considered secrets and in some cases veiled in allegory, they are still right in front of your face. Through deep thought and reflection on your own experiences, in conjunction with the experiences of the many who have walked the path you have yet to walk, the light on that path can become brighter.

It is up to you to decide if you are ready to master the game. It is up to you to decide if you are ready to win the game. The game of life has been, and will always be there waiting for you to play. You are in it for life.

15

Tenets

In life, we should all have self governing rules by which we live. These rules should be personally instituted and inculcated by ourselves, for ourselves and to ourselves. Integrity, honor, morality, honesty, loyalty, respect, dignity, fidelity, humility, self–esteem, self–respect, self–discipline, perseverance, tenacity, principle, character, decency, fortitude, firmness, patience, ethics, distinction, sincerity, brotherly love, relief and truth are just some of the tenets I have chosen to try and live by.

Tenets and principles are what builds character. It is up to you to decide which path is for you and which path is not for you. Character can be good and it can be bad. Depending on the environment you may find yourself in, the peers you choose to be around and the social atmosphere of your surroundings, your character will be a reflection of that and more. Fortunately for you, most of what makes up a good or bad character can be controlled. Having a good character is just one of the many tenets that you should strive to achieve.

As a member of the Boy Scouts of America, I was taught many tenets. We learned to recite various principles that I will always be able to recite such as: A Scout is trustworthy, loyal, helpful, friendly, courteous, kind, obedient, cheerful, thrifty, brave, clean and reverent. That was the scout law that all young scouts had to learn. For many of us, we even had to learn the real meanings behind the words. The meanings to such words are what helps to instill character in young men.

Trustworthy: A Scout tells the truth. He keeps his promises. Honesty is part of his code of conduct. People can depend on him.

Loyal: A Scout is true to his family, Scout leaders, friends, school, and nation.

Helpful: A Scout is concerned about other people. He does things willingly for others without pay or reward.

Friendly: A Scout is a friend to all. He is a brother to other Scouts. He seeks to understand others. He respects those with ideas and customs other than his own.

Courteous: A Scout is polite to everyone regardless of age or position. He knows good manners makes it easier for people to get along together.

Kind: A Scout understands that there is strength in being gentle. He treats others as he wants to be treated. He does not hurt or kill harmless things without reason.

Obedient: A Scout follows the rules of his family, school, and troop. He obeys the laws of his community and country. If he thinks these rules and laws are unfair, he tries to have them changed in an orderly manner rather than disobey them.

Cheerful: A scout looks for the bright side of things. He cheerfully does tasks that come his way. He tries to make others happy.

Thrifty: A Scout works to pay his way and to help others. He saves for unforeseen needs. He protects and conserves natural resources. He carefully uses time and property.

Brave: A Scout can face danger even if he is afraid. He has the courage to stand for what he thinks is right even if others laugh at or threaten him.

Clean: A Scout keeps his body and mind fit and clean. He goes around with those who believe in living by these same ideals. He helps keep his home and community clean.

Reverent: A Scout is reverent towards God. He is faithful in his religious duties. He respects the beliefs of others.

These are just a few of the types of tenets that I learned from scouting. It is no wonder that many scholarship applications ask if you were in scouting. It is no wonder that you are given a court of honor when you attain the highest rank, that being an Eagle Scout. It is no wonder you receive an award of recognition from the President of the United States when you earn the rank of Eagle. You possess the character that makes real leaders.

As you go through life, you will have the fortune to observe many tenets in action. Some tenets will stick with you and some will not.

You will even attach yourself to some tenets with such strong convictions, you may adopt them as tenets to live by. The principles by which you govern your life will become closely identified with your character as you grow older. It will be what makes you, you. Whether it is negative or positive, as you live within these tenets, so shall these tenets live within you. These tenets will begin to create an aura around you that will be able to be seen and felt by others. This is when you will be able to sum up the most closely related characteristics about yourself in one word.

Another characteristic that many people try to attain is self discipline. Also, one of the most admired characteristics in a person is self discipline. In life we have many things we need to do. Equally, we have many distractions which could prevent us from doing those things. It takes self discipline to learn martial arts and achieve the black belt level. It takes self discipline to earn the rank of Eagle in scouting. It takes self discipline to complete a college degree with honors. Likewise it takes a tremendous amount of self discipline, along with tenacity to achieve your dreams and aspirations in life. Things do not just happen by themselves, you have to make them happen. With self discipline, you can achieve whatever your dreams may be.

Along with self discipline, you must maintain your self esteem. As long as you know who you are, no one can change you into anything else. You will not be prone to follow the crowd, trying to find your identity, because you already have it. You will not be victimized by peer pressure because your self esteem will protect you. True knowledge of who you are, where you have come from and where you are going, will help to build your self esteem as opposed to allowing it to be torn down. When you really know who you are, you have something that cannot be taken away from you. That is your essence. Only you should control your essence. Through self esteem, you will always be in control.

Son, there are lots of philosophies that I would like to pass on to you. Hopefully in time I will. In stating the various tenets I feel closely related to at the beginning of the chapter, I highly recommend you research each of them to get a deeper understanding of their meanings. The one that I have grown closest to, the one that I feel is the most important one for me to live by and the one that challenges me as a man to continually walk upright on the straight path, is <u>Integrity</u>.

To me integrity is the most important tenet to live by. From integrity flows honor which allows me to hold my head up high in any situation. From integrity emerges truth; this is the highest maxim of art and of life, the secrete of virtue, and of all moral authority.

Not all men have integrity. As a matter of fact, I will go so far as to say that many men do not have integrity. It is hard work to have integrity. It is the ability to say the right thing and do the right thing even though you know the consequences will be unfavorable. Integrity is when you inconvenience your own self because of your convictions. Do unto others, as you would have others do unto you is easy to say; but the man that can live it, is truly a remarkable man. It is not easy living the eloquent words dictating righteousness. Integrity has many meanings, but above all, it means doing the right thing. In most cases the easiest thing to do may not always be the right thing to do. In many cases the right thing to do may not always be the best thing to do. In some cases what you consider the best thing to do might not be what others consider the best thing to do. It is not easy having integrity.

Although you can buy many things, and certainly everything has its price, you cannot buy integrity. You can only pay with it. Because of integrity, our forefathers never lost sight of freedom. Because of integrity, many of our ancestral fathers, mothers and children were killed. It is said, "If a man has nothing worth dying for, he has nothing worth living for." This is integrity at its highest pinnacle. This is the price that has been paid all too many times.

Integrity not only challenges you, it makes you challenge yourself. Since we are all human beings, none of us is perfect in any manner. We all have weaknesses and frailties. When someone offers you a healthy bribe that the average person would gladly accept, integrity makes you turn down that bribe. When an illegal opportunity to acquire wealth or assets without anyone knowing it but you arises, it is integrity that helps you to resist the opportunity. Even if you should give in to one of the many negative temptations, if you do have integrity, you will be constantly trying to right your wrongs.

While I have attempted to give you an understanding about integrity, I could never fully explain it. Integrity is something you feel, it is something you witness, it is something to be admired. You cannot receive it, neither can you impart it, however, you can and should develop it.

How you live your life is what makes you who you are. Your tenets are the seeds that will some day blossom. Just as there are some plants that are not the most pleasing to look at or be around, so are there people. Equally there are a variety of plants that are extremely desirable to look at, to be around, to touch, to smell, to revere; so too are there people.

<u>Wisely choose the tenets you wish to follow.</u>

16

Education

It is very difficult to explain education. Even though I have a Bachelor of Science degree in Education, I have come to realize that Pythagoras was right in saying, "The more you learn, the more you realize how little you know." I used to think that education was a form of training, until I learned what training was and dismissed my former thoughts. However, I have learned that education has to do with bringing out that which is already in us. As Dr. Na'im Akbar put it, "Moving in accord with our pre–determined nature is the nature of education."

When you are taught, "In 1492 Christopher Columbus sailed the ocean blue and discovered America," you are not being educated, you are being trained; you are being mis–educated. When a hawk flies out and catches his prey to feed himself and his young, he is educated. When that same hawk flies off of a man's arm and kills prey for that man, only to receive a reward, he is trained, he is mis–educated, he is a servant, he is a slave.

When you manifest what you already are—what is already inside of you, you are being educated. It is when you are trying to be something or develop something that someone else wants you to be, that you are actually being trained. Your education lies within your identity. If you have an identity, and you know who you are, then you can be educated. If you do not have and identity, and you do not know yourself, then you will probably be trained, not educated.

Before there were universities, colleges, great hallowed learning institutions, computers, television, radio, and books, there was education. Before there was civilization, there was uncivilization and during the time of uncivilization, there was education.

As human beings, we are all blessed creatures because we are not restricted by instinct. The way you are able to find out what you have to do, is by learning, by developing your consciousness, by beginning to study yourself, by studying all the rest of creation, by studying your history as a human being, and in the process, discovering patterns which dignify and make you what you are. That is what education is supposed to do. It is supposed to provide you with the knowledge about yourself, so that you can be what you are supposed to be.

Your education comes from many things. You are educated by fish, insects, animals, reptiles, and birds. How else do you think man conceived building a boat, a car, an airplane, a submarine, a helicopter, etc. By observing fish, man has developed aquatic products such as boats, fins and diving gear. By studying creatures which move across the earth faster than man like the horse, man has developed the car. By the fascination of birds, man learned the various theories of lift and drag and brought forth the aerospace industry. These inventions and developments were not conceived just from thought. Through educational stimulation and observation of God's creation, man has been able to develop what has always been around us.

Many martial arts techniques which dates as far back as 2600 BC, also come from animals. The ancient practitioners would study the movements of animals and develop new techniques from their observation. You can also learn a lot from flowers, fruits, trees and other plants. It is ironic to hear people refer to <u>family tree</u> or their <u>roots</u> when discussing their lineage. Your education will manifest itself through the study of stones, metals and gems. Equally will you be educated from the study of the earth, water, air and fire. Whether you are reflecting on the celestial or the terrestrial, through education you can see things and say, "Why not?"

As you progress through your education by way of school, you will encounter many subjects. English, history, language, reading, writing, etc. are just some of the subjects you will be challenged with. All of these subjects can be conquered with relative ease or difficulty; it is all in your state of mind. If you think you can, you will, if you think you dare not, you will not. All that is being taught was manifested in someone. That means that there is nothing being taught that you do not already possess. You just have to develop it. Once you begin to develop it, school (no matter what the level) becomes easier. It becomes a game that you are able to win. You just have to learn the rules and understand them.

Of the many arts and sciences you will be challenged with, there are seven in particular which I feel are very important for you to learn. These seven will help to unlock the key to any other subject you may encounter. Grammar, rhetoric, logic, arithmetic, geometry, music and astronomy will all prove useful to you as you progress through life.

Grammar teaches us to express our thoughts in appropriate words, which are beautified and adorned by rhetoric. Logic is the means by which we think and reason in proportion, and make language subordinate to thought. Arithmetic is the science of computing numbers. Geometry treats of the powers, proportion and magnitude in general where length, breadth, and thickness are considered from a point to a line, from a line to a superficies, from a superficies to a solid. A point is the beginning of all geometrical matter; a line is the continuation of the same; a superficies is the length and breadth without the given thickness, a solid is the length and breadth with the given thickness, which forms a cube and comprehends the whole of the science of geometry.

Music teaches the art of forming concord, so as to compose delightful harmony by a mathematical and proportional arrangement of acute, grave and mixed sounds. This art, by a series of experiments, is reduced to a demonstrative science, with respect to tone and intervals of sound.

Astronomy is that divine art which inspired the contemplative mind to soar aloft and read the wisdom, strength and beauty of the Almighty Creator. By astronomy we can observe the motions, measure the distance, comprehend the magnitude and calculate the periods and eclipses of the heavenly bodies.

Once you have learned these arts and sciences, learning the rest will be as easy as being born. All you have to do is allow nature to take its course. In learning the various subjects that you will be challenged with, do not be disillusioned into thinking that the more education you have, the more money you can make. Do not feel that because you are a college graduate, you are now entitled to something more than the non–graduate. And please do not entertain the myth that because you have an academic education, you are better than someone. That would be a monumental mistake on your part.

There are people who have never even set foot in college, yet they are, in many respects, just as educated as you are. While growing up, it was not uncommon to hear someone tell me that they never made it pass the 6th grade. When I was an instructor at a place called Educational Services, an educational institution where people go to get prepared to take their GED test, I had many students who were older than me. I think my oldest student was 76 years old. She was an ordained minister and wrote some of the best papers in the class. When I taught English and history, she had all the answers. When I taught chemistry she told me she was too old to be thinking about being a scientist so she got a "B".

While teaching there, I think I learned more from them than they did from me. I taught them book history to pass the test and they taught me life's history to survive in this world. They remembered the 30's, 40's, 50's 60's and 70's as if it were yesterday. There were times when I needed to expound on a subject in history and I would just turn the class over to them for a while. Not only did I learn from those people who did not even have a high school education, but they also made teaching a real pleasure. So, if ever you think that you are smarter than someone because you read a book, be careful, they may have known the author.

READING

Reading can either be a chore or a pleasure, it all depends on how you approach it and how you prepared and equipped yourself before reading. Too many of us do not read enough. As a matter of fact, there is a joke about Blacks which is sad, but often true. "If you want to keep a secret from a Black man, put it in a book." That is a sad statement; however, in order for such a statement to be perpetuated, the facts must first exist. Do not let these facts apply to you.

Personally, when I first heard that statement, I immediately did a self evaluation to determine if it applied to me. After realizing that I was guilty of not reading enough, I began a journey to correct my flaw. I also shared that comment with many of my friends, both black and white so that they too could do a self evaluation as I had done. The results translated into self development. The more you read, the more you learn. The more you learn, the wiser you become. The wiser you become, the stronger you are. This evolutional educational process will give you powers which will enable you to do things you never thought were possible.

When you read a book, it is like taking a journey to another land. You get to experience things you never would have experienced if you had stayed home. You get to enjoy learning from others who have also read books. This is why knowledge is so vast. If I am able to write this book after reading over 3000 books throughout my lifetime; and each author of the books I have read also read 3000 books, that means that by reading this book, you are receiving over 9 million books worth of information. In actuality, the figures would be infinite, because the number of generations of past readers and authors is an unknown. Nevertheless, this knowledge is not a secret. It is there for all who desires it. You just have to read.

In this book I hope I have stimulated all sorts of thoughts in your mind. In some cases I hoped to challenge you to challenge me. Question whether I am telling the truth or just making this stuff up. Perhaps there are things I have said in this book that you find difficult to believe. Perhaps I said something in this book which you took offense to. Whatever thoughts, emotions, accolades or disagreements you may have, remember, I wrote this book by way of the knowledge I have gained from reading other books and the experiences I have encountered. So before you challenge or even agree with me, Read! This is only one book. You have 2999 more to go.

 **DICTIONARY** To grasp a small understanding about how much knowledge there is for you to pursue, consider that every word has a definition. Also consider that each sentence has lots of words which increase the sentence's definition. Looking at paragraphs with lots of sentences increases the information base from just a word definition to a wealth of information. Putting ten to twenty paragraphs together, you now have an article. Put over fifty paragraphs together, you have a small book. This particular book has about 60,000 words, and each word has at least one

definition, that translates into a wealth of information. After reading it, then it translates into a wealth of knowledge. This knowledge grows every time you read.

To be well read is to be well versed, to be illiterate is to be well cursed.

THE EDUCATIONAL SYSTEM

As for our educational system, it has many flaws. Every time I read the educational journal or something else pertaining to the system of education, it seems that they are always talking about revamping the educational system. That clearly tells me that something is wrong if they are constantly trying to revamp a system.

Initially our present school system, as we know it, was designed to conform to the industrial age. It was and still is an assembly line process. You begin by receiving certain skills and tools. You are passed on to the next stage every June to begin a new process in September. Almost every student in the United States goes through this process for at least 12 years of their life. At the end of the journey you get a seal of approval in the form of a diploma. This does not mean you are educated or smart in any way shape or form, it means you have completed the assembly line process outlined by the government.

Suppose one of those students in the assembly line process had the potential to be a CEO of an express mail company. He would never be recognized because the system is not designed to recognize him. As with the assembly line, if a part is bad, they just get rid of it rather than try to figure out why it is bad. It is not until after the parts are being thrown out on a frequent basis that someone recognizes that there may be a problem. Usually by that time it is too late to correct the problem, and the entire operation has to be shut down and rebuilt.

This same analogy can be applied to the school. As long as only a few students where being failed, suspended, expelled, transferred, given remedial training (left back), etc, the system kept right on moving. As long as only the high percentages of students who where victims were

minorities, the system kept right on moving. Now that there are igno-
rant, uneducated, illiterate and incognizant high school graduates
destroying our country, because that is all they know and understand,
people are beginning to see that there is a grave problem. Unfortunately in this case, the people responsible for its destruction are not
qualified to fix it. They just do not have the vision or education.

A simple test to determine if someone has the ability and qualifica-
tions to fix our educational system is to see if they head straight for statistics. If they do, they are not qualified. They are just going to do what
has always been done. Spend a few million dollars on a statistical study,
show some charts and figures as a result of the statistics, and come up
with a billion dollar solution that will take at least five years for some
more statistics to determine if it worked. Meanwhile another decade
with another generation is lost to a statistic.

It has become customary for the United States to play the numbers
game with almost everything we do. We have statistics for everything.
Look at the results of the SAT test for the nation, the east coast vs. west
coast, males vs. females, private school vs. public school, etc. Why do
we have these statistics? After denying so many people the opportunity
to attend various colleges because they did not score as high as the statistics say they needed to score in order to do well in school, the system
is now taking a look at the whole person concept. The system is also
looking at changing the SAT test all together because it is now being
determined that the SAT test is culturally biased. How long did the
statistics take to determine that? For every year that passes, we actually
become more culturally aware. That means that for every year we go
backwards, we were less culturally aware. If that is the case, those who
took the SAT's in the 70's were deceived. How can they be compen-
sated for such a mistake? Did I say mistake? Perhaps it was systemati-
cally done. Maybe it was just overlooked. In any event, it does not take
a statistical analysis to determine the effects. It is obvious.

It is also obvious what needs to be done to the educational system.
We need to teach the truth and teach students how to think for them-

selves. We need to start producing thinkers and philosophers not just graduates. If you help students to develop their abilities to use what they already have inside of themselves, the system will never get out of hand. The students will begin to put their teachers in check for their errors and malpractice. The students will begin demanding that the out dated books and lesson plans be discarded and replaced with updated and correct material. The students will be calling for the resignation of those who they feel are not competent and capable of teaching because they will have been taught how to weed out incompetents. However, when you teach that children should be seen and not heard, you have just placed gasoline on the fire rather than water.

TEACH YOURSELF

Although our institutions are supposed to teach us what we need to know about many things, never rely solely on someone or something else to teach you what you need to know. You have to also teach yourself. My brother once corrected a biology teacher in high school because the biology teacher stated several incorrect facts. The biology teacher took offense and said to my brother if he thinks he can do a better job, why does he not teach the class? My brother being the intelligent person he was, got up and began instructing the class. The teacher made him sit down, after realizing that he was very capable of teaching the class.

What the teacher did not realize however, was that my brother read the entire biology text book from cover to cover when he first received it. I think it took him about a month. As the teacher taught the various sections and assigned various chapters, it was all just review for my brother. He was keeping up with the teacher, rather than just keeping up with the class, because he felt the class was too slow for him. He did this with all his classes and of course got all A's. (with the exception of biology class) However, after my mother got involved and the principal finished his investigation, he received his A in biology.

I learned a lot from my younger brother about education. I remembered he used to read the encyclopedias at home. He began with the A book and read straight through to Z. Back then we used to think he was weird. I look back on those days and now I see he was a genius. The one thing I learned from reflecting on the way my brother strategized his game plan on education is, he was always in control. He never wanted anyone to have control over his education. Even if he did not get along with a teacher, he did not give the teacher the satisfaction of having control over his grades. He excelled better than everyone in the class in such an obvious manner. If the teacher even thought about hurting his grades, he had a defense. It is imperative that you take full control of your education. The teachers, instructors and professors are all there to serve you. You are not there to serve them.

If you put your academic education in the hands of your teachers, you will only go as far as your teacher will allow you to go. If you take full control of your education, then you can go as far as you want to go.

As an Air Force Recruiter, I interviewed more dropouts and unqualified people than I interviewed qualified people. That was because the students did not take control of their education. They allowed the system, which is based on the assembly line and statistics, to give them what the statistics said they should have. Nothing... They had nothing. The simple question I used to ask was, "If a man walked one mile in one hour, how fast did he walk?" More people got that answer wrong than right, and they were either high school seniors or graduates. Do not rely on the system. Rely on yourself.

PAY NOW—PLAY LATER

For those who do know how to use the system, beat the system, cheat the system, bypass the system, or fool the system, they get to go to the next level. It would be wise to have the educational tools you are supposed to have when meeting challenges that require you to know your stuff. If not, you will have to go back and get it like I had to.

It is embarrassing, and also a waste of time, to have to go through remedial math and English in college; however I had to do it. I was on a 7th grade reading level and I could not do algebra when I went to my first college. It was not that I was dumb or stupid or anything like that. I just had not taken control of my education. Needless to say, I have since corrected that mistake; and I must admit, it was a high price to pay. If it were not for the spell check of the computer, you would see how high a price I am still paying.

Since then I have come up with a theory which I have shared in many of my speeches and lectures. I call it the pay now, play later theory. If you play now at the younger stages and not take control of your education, you will be paying for the rest of your life. You will be constantly looking back on your mistakes wishing you had another chance to do it better. This applies to many other areas besides education. You have to pay your dues no matter what you are doing. If you do not pay your dues when you should, you will pay them later, only with interest.

You will be paying for the rest of your life for the few years you neglected to pay when you should have. Equally, if you are wise and you do pay now, you do decide to take control of your education and you arm yourself with the tools you will need later, you will be able to play for the rest of your life at a level many only dream about.

Your educational growth is just that, yours. An Air Force supervisor of mines used to always tell me, "Your career is a self–help program." Do not rely on anyone. Do not allow someone else to control it. As Carter G. Woodson used to say, "When you control a man's thinking, you do not have to worry about his actions. You do not have to tell him to stand here or go yonder. He will find his <u>proper place</u> and will stay in it. You do not need to send him to the back door. He will go without being told. In fact, if there is no back door, he will cut one for his special benefit. His education makes it necessary."

FINAL WORDS

This information about education I have shared with you is all around you, and it is in you. All you have to do is manifest it. Bring out the greatest which is in you and you shall see your true identity. When you begin to see and understand that which lies within you, not only will you be educated, you will then become the educator.

17

Ethnic Origin

The subject of ethnic origin, minorities, prejudice, color, race, etc., has been and always will be a problem. I have had to deal with this subject my entire life, and so will you. I have tried to answer the question, "Why" and have come up with an answer that has satisfied me for over fourteen years. The question: Why is why the way it is? The answer: Because that is the way it is and always will be. I have listened to idealistic speeches and promises time after time, and none of them have solved the problem, nor will they ever. I have watched program after program instituted to solve the problem of race, prejudice, etc., and they seem to get replaced with something else, because the initial one did not work. As long as there remains one person with opposing views, the problem never will be solved.

The military was one of the most racist environments I have ever experienced. Depending on the prevailing ethnic group, that group would determine the ethnic tone of the section. If it were predominantly black, then the black ethnic group would dominate in the language spoken, the music played, the attitudes, and the sports the base supported. If the group were predominantly white or Mexican, then that group traits and environmental history would be the dominating factor.

The new rules and regulations did not stop the thugs from acting like thugs. It did not stop the red necks from acting like red necks. It did not stop the good ole boy network from operating and promoting the ones it wanted to promote, it just gave the game a new twist. As we used to say in my old neighborhood "You can take the boy out of the streets, but you can't take the street out of the boy." Although I can step in and out of various environments, I will always remember what I learned from the streets, so that saying is true in my case.

Even in many areas where fair and equitable treatment was supposed to be the prevailing factor, like making rank through the promotional system, receiving awards and decorations for outstanding service, and even receiving local recognition for outstanding performance, discrimination was obvious. I can recall all too often when I consistently came in second place for various competitions in the Air Force. Even my white counterparts who observed the competition, and some who competed against me, told me something was wrong. Although no one would openly admit it, discrimination was the reason for my consistent second place position. For some reason, the decision makers just could not bring themselves to allow a Black to be superior.

Although there were many times when I came in first place for various monthly, quarterly and yearly awards, to include even winning two honor graduate awards, I was, in most cases, the only Black to receive the recognition. This was a very strange feeling when I was among my peers. The whites were very angry at me because I was black, and the Blacks were angry because they thought I did something underhanded (brown–nosed) to get the recognition.

After receiving this cold shoulder type of treatment, I began doing a little research to find out if in fact the military was discriminating against Blacks. I began tuning into reality with a different level of awareness, and the reality was all around me. There were no black Generals at the base, there were no black senior Non–Commissioned officers out of the entire Aircraft section, and there was not one black Commander anywhere for me to ask questions. This was a strange feeling. I even began looking at the list of award recipients for the years past; the names with the exception of mine were all white. I started analyzing the high level award recipients and positions received from that day forward, and it was a clear signal to me that something was wrong. Even some of my white friends admitted to the racial discrimination they witnessed.

After learning how significant the racial discrimination was, I decided to do something about correcting it. I joined the rod and gun club, which was 100% white, and was surprised to see how accepted I was. Although this club was clearly a group of red necks doing their thing, they had nothing personal against me. They accepted me into the club with all the rights and privileges afforded to anyone who wanted to join. They taught me how to shoot skeet and trap and a few other events. This led me to believe that they were not 100% at fault, as I had believed. The problem here was that no Blacks had ever applied to join the club. Although they remained red necks and kept their good ole boy attitude, they did not treat me like a "BOY." They gave me the respect I deserved and commanded as a Man.

The bottom line is that you are who you are, and that is just the way it is. Nevertheless, that does not give anyone the right to disgrace and discriminate against you simply because of your color or ethnic origin. Because a person is different, does not make him any better or worse than you are. Because traditionally Blacks were slaves does not mean it was right. Equally, because Blacks were enslaved by whites long ago does not mean you should hold the whites of present day accountable for what happened in the past. Wrong is wrong! We are all different and we should all be afforded the same opportunities to achieve and succeed in this world, based on our own initiatives. You cannot expect people to change simply because you want them to, nor should you change simply because someone else wants you to. Be yourself.

Now there are some obvious things that occurred which has tipped the scale in the favor of the whites. Having plantations which could be handed down from generation to generation is a very good start. As a matter of fact, in 200 years time, posterity has numbered into the hundreds, which means lots of potential millionaires. It also means that all the close friends of the plantation owners and their heirs would be equally positioned to be comfortable. If my great, great, great grandfather owned one half of a state, perhaps life would have turned out different for me. If my mother and all of my aunts and uncles owned forty acres and a mule, then I am sure life would have been different for me.

If Congressmen, Senators, Governors, Mayors, etc, do not have to give up their seat every year, then it is no wonder it took so long for Blacks and other minorities to get a few crumbs from the pie. General Electric, Ford, McDonnell Douglas, Boeing, Dupont, and many more still have the largest shares of that pie, and their families were not black. Look at the percentage of Blacks in congress or the percentage of Blacks you see on television sitting in the press section during press conferences. It is very obvious that we are under represented. And let us not forget the Presidency. It seems that every time a president appoints someone black into a position of power, it is a big deal. Why? I will bet that when there is finally a black president, everyone will be making such a big deal of it, he will not be able to do his job properly. Look at South Africa, it is evolutionally and biologically impossible for a person with white skin to evolve in that much sun, yet it seems like a big deal for them to have a black president. That is the way it should be. South Africa should be ruled by someone of a dark complexion.

The bottom line is that Blacks are finally being allowed to come to the starting block of the race after the race has already been going on. If you were to run a 50 mile race and found out everyone had begun running before you even got out of bed that morning, you would say that it is not fair. If by the time you got to the starting block of the race, you heard that the closest person to you was already at the 20 mile marker, you would be discouraged. This is reality, and that is just the way it is. You can sit there complaining about how impossible it will be for you to win the race, or you can start running as fast as you can.

It is very obvious from that scenario, that you have no chance of winning the race; but through education, through knowledge, and through vision, you will see things that never were and say, "Why Not?" Why not run in the race anyway? You may not win, but you can finish. If you never finish the first race, how can you win the second, third and so forth. This is the way you have to deal with the adversities and strikes that are already against you. You have to get into the race and run. What has happened in the past cannot be changed, however, you can change the course of the future. Just by finishing one race, you pave the way for more runners to be there at the beginning.

Hank Aaron, Jesse Jackson, Arsenio Hall, Joseph E. Marshall, Jr., Muhammad Ali, Crispus Attucks, Frederick Douglas, Richard Prior, Martin Luther King Jr., Thurgood Marshall, Booker T. Washington, James Brown, Denzel Washington, Areatha Franklin, Huey Newton, Sharon Pratt Dixon, Andrew Young, Maya Angelou, James Baldwin, Toni Morrison, Bryant Gumbel, James Earl Jones, Louis Armstrong, Oprah Winfrey, Benjamin S. Carson, Sr., M.D., Judge Calvin T. Wilson, Calvin T. Wilson II, M.D., Branford Marsalis, Ed Bradley, Rosa Parks, Prince, Michael Jackson, Willi Smith, Kareem Abdul–Jabbar, Quincy Jones, Michael Jordan, Jim Brown, Redd Foxx, Eddie Murphy, Marion Van Peoples, Walter Payton, Joe Louis, Malcolm X, Henry Austin, Spike Lee, General Benjamin O. Davis Sr. and Jr., General Colin L. Powell, William Bullock, Mary E. Bullock, Clemon Bullock, Sam Bullock, Solomon H. Bullock, Johnny Bullock, Calvin Bullock, Priscilla Bullock, Annie Bullock, Eunice Bullock, Josephine Bullock, Jean Bullock, Martha Bullock, Jessie Bullock, Maude Bullock, Mary M. Bullock, Clara Bullock, and millions more, have paved the way for new runners. It is your duty, and your responsibility to continue the race. Either you will pave the way for the next generation, or you will win the race.

This is how you should deal with the subject of race as it relates to your achieving whatever it is you are capable of achieving. I talked about it in the chapter on struggles, I talked about it in the chapter on games, I talked about it in the chapter on education; you have to beat the odds.

In relation to your specific ethnic origin, all I can say is: learn all you can. Although I am strongly against race discrimination, I feel that racial/ethnic pride is necessary. You need to know where you came from. You need to know the history of your ancestors. You need to know what have become common words like "Picnic" mean. You need to understand the atrocities of slavery. It is all necessary for your development as a person. It is said, "Those who do not learn from their past are doomed to repeat it." If you take a close look at our class structure, you will see that there are many people repeating the past. Why? Because they did not learn from it.

We, as a people, need to learn to live together no mater what color, race, religion, creed or ethnic origin we are. Although this world will never accomplish that task as a whole, you can as an individual. Judge people by the content of their character, not by the color of their skin. If their content reveals a raciest bigot, then that is how you deal with them. If they reveal a good heart and an open mind, then that is the level you should reciprocate at.

I have friends from all sorts of ethnic origins. I have friends in England, Saudi Arabia, Spain, Germany, Switzerland, New Zealand, Australia, India, Egypt, South America, Canada, Italy, Israel, Bangladesh, Turkey, Africa and other countries, and we get along fine. I have white friends who have treated me better than some of the black people that have betrayed me. It is the character of a person which should be judged, not their group. If you judge a person by their group, you are no better than the ones who discriminate against you.

Although I have been and continue to be discriminated against by whites, I cannot allow myself to formulate an opinion which brings me right down to their level. Although I have been and continue to go into stores which have only white Barbie Dolls for sale by the hundreds and no other ethnic dolls, I cannot allow myself to hate all the merchants. Although I have worked for a company and have seen others celebrate every holiday the card companies tell them to celebrate, yet Black History month goes totally unnoticed, I cannot hold that against my co-workers. Although I am familiar with the many burnings of African Americans as a Sunday after church activity, and allowed by local and state governments, where the burned body parts were auctioned in fun, I still cannot hold all white people accountable for the actions of their relatives.

It takes a strong man to be able to stand up against all the odds and achieve what he is capable of achieving. It takes a strong man to be able to feel the flame of the fire and the sting of the whip and not cry out for help from the oppressor. It takes a strong man to redefine the barriers that have kept people from progressing. It takes strength to see and understand how to deal with the problems that you will face all of your life because of your ethnic origin. Through strength, you will find the solutions to the many problems that have yet to confront you because of your ethnic origin. Never forget, you are not alone. Never forget, millions have helped to clear the path so that you may win the race.

18

Life and Death

This world has been built by trillions of hands and minds. The Stone Hinge, the Pyramids, irrigation systems, bridges, books, maps, machines, languages, music, art, aircraft, computers, hospitals, medicine, technologies and science, are all contributions from people who impacted this world. Imagine if no one was ever interested in discovering math. We would still be at a very primitive state, yet some people refuse to even learn it. The hard part was discovering it, the easy part is learning it.

How are you impacting the world in which you live? How are you impacting the people you come in contact with? What contributions will you be remembered for after you are gone? The answers to these questions can only be answered by you. Only you hold the power. There is an old Native American story that was related to me many moons ago when I was a young camper that I would like to share, which explains the power you hold.

One year a Native American tribal chief wanted to select his successor. He assembled all of his warriors and gave them all sorts of tasks to eliminate the unworthy. After several months had passed he narrowed the competition down to the two best warriors. Both wanted to be chief, however, they needed to prove their true power to the chief, which would be the final test.

He commanded both to venture up to the mountains and bring back an eagle's egg from the nest of an eagle. The two departed and returned one week later with their egg. The chief examined both eggs and ordered both warriors to demonstrate their true powers to the entire tribe. The first warrior let out a loud scream, held the egg up in the air and crushed it with all of his might. The next warrior wrapped the egg in cloth to keep it warm, and returned the egg back to the nest from which he took it.

After the warriors returned, the chief asked them both to explain why they made the decisions they made. The first warrior spoke boldly that he was the most powerful warrior in the tribe. Since the eagle was regarded as the most superior bird of the air, by destroying the egg, he gained the powers of the eagle. The second warrior said that he too felt that he was the most powerful warrior in the tribe, however, he was also compassionate and merciful. He felt true power was the gift of giving life, not destroying it. By returning the egg to the nest, he was giving life which would in turn give more life. Hearing this, the chief proclaimed the second warrior as his successor.

It is not certain how long your life will last. Your life could end before you finish this book, this paragraph or even the breath you have just unconsciously taken in. What is certain, is that you are alive now and you should try to live life to the fullest. I have a saying that was passed on to me. "Live life as if each day was your last, then after that, live as if you were going to live forever." If you were to die today, you will have lived. As the saying goes, tomorrow is not promised to any of us.

Death is something that is definite, absolute and final. You are born, you live and you die. These three things are inseparable and inevitable. And although death has been going on since the beginning of life, we still have problems dealing with it. Perhaps it is the value system we are brought up with. Perhaps it is the denial attitudes we witness. Perhaps it is the media. Whatever the reason, death is all around you and one day your turn will come. It is a fact of life that cannot be denied or evaded.

I am not going to tell you how to feel about death because you can only feel it when you see or experience it. Although all the holy books explain death and teach that it is a part of life, for some reason most of the so–called religious people forget that part when someone close to them dies. Your mind might tell you the logical thing to do or feel, however, your emotions do not always listen to your mind and you express yourself based on how you really feel.

I have experienced death from close friends to relatives, and it is different every time. The more I experience it, the more I am able to understand it. The more I am able to understand it, the easier it is to accept it. That may or may not work for you.

My brother, whom I spoke of earlier in the book, committed suicide. While an engineering major at Massachusetts Institute of Technology (M.I.T.) in his second year, he hung himself in his dorm room. He wrote a very descriptive last will and testament. He also stated why he was taking his life. I was stationed in the Air Force in Germany when I got the news which devastated me. He was about 15 months younger than I was and we were very close. I cried, I yelled, I punched things and I did a lot of thinking. It was very difficult. My First Sergeant told me something that has stuck with me that I share with other people who are grieving. He said, "The pain never goes away, it just lessens over a period of time." He was right. I related that truthful statement to my wife when she lost her father and to several other friends, and it seems that, that statement has held true.

Just as life is one big learning experience, so is death. Every time you experience someone close to you dying, you learn something. You learn something about yourself and you learn something about life. It forces you to do an introspection. Through introspection you are able to think at a level that is not always easy to do on a regular basis. It sometimes requires a transient like state of mind so that you are able to access your subconscience thoughts and use them to answer the questions you seek answers to. In many cases, experiencing a death can put you in that frame of thought. How you come out of it is up to you.

Presently we are going through an era of clashing value systems which is challenging our government and court systems more than ever. Abortions, the right to life, death with dignity and capital punishment are just a few of the issues which revolve around death. How quickly we forget that this same government used to burn so called witches at the stake. This same government used to hang the criminals regularly, in public, and many were innocent. This same government who is frowning on a young man getting caned for vandalism, used to whip human beings by the thousands, daily, and rejoice about it. This same government used to burn Blacks as a Sunday after church outing and then auctioned the burned body parts to men, women and children. So called, good Christians. It is no wonder we do not understand death.

It was not too long ago that Blacks were victims of the police force on a scale that I call genocide. They shot into crowds of blacks at will, killing as many as they could. They turned their attack dogs loose on them happily. They bombed their houses, burned their churches, ripped the skin right of off their bones with high pressure water hoses and more. This was all considered normal not too long ago. I bet that there are many people who could tell you all about those days first hand. Just ask them.

Our past allows us to move into the future with an understanding of that which has worked and that which has not. With this understanding, we are now able to understand death better than we did in our past. In the stone age, when a person died, I am sure there were a lot of unanswered questions. Hopefully here in the technological age, we have been able to answer some of those questions.

Life and death comes and goes. We must try to look beyond the trained values to begin to understand the unknown. It is that unknown which holds the key to the many answers to the questions we seek. What is life? Why is there life? Is their life after death? No one person can give you the answers. No one person knows all the answers. Whether you choose to believe or not to believe what ever you are told is your prerogative. There is one fact that is true, and to this you can believe. You are born, you live and you die.

Make the best of the life you have been blessed with...

19

Words To Live By

The following are phrases and quotes that I have heard, read, remembered, and in some cases, written myself that I feel would be useful to you. Some are thought provoking, direct, and a few, controversial. Nevertheless, you can learn something from each one of these phrases.

1. It's one thing to tuck your child into bed, but it's the after tuck that counts. R.B.

2. Always remember what it is like to be poor...

3. If you want to keep a secret from a black man, put it in a book.

4. Always try to know as much about what you are getting into before you get into it. It helps you stay in it. R.B.

5. Had I known then, what I know now, I would have done it differently.

6. The best thing you can spend on a child is time.

7. Never volunteer information.

8. The greatest ignorance is to reject something you know nothing about...

9. You have two choices: either kiss my ass, or kick it. R.B.

10. You are a product of your environment; however, through education, you can become a product of your knowledge. R.B.

11. The more you learn, the more you realize how little you know. (Phythagorous)

12. The difference between winners and losers is, winners are willing to do the things that losers aren't willing to do.

13. Never make a promise you can't keep.

14. We all do the same things; what makes us different is the way we do them.

15. Reach for the stars, even if you only touch the sun, you've still made it.

16. "It is a rare man who can calm a hush upon the world while they listen to him speak." R.B.

17. "You can pay now and play later –or– you can play now and pay for the rest of your life" R.B.

18. Never send a boy to do a man's job, he'll just come back a boy, whereas a man will come back with results. R.B.

19. Believe half of what you see, nothing of what you hear, and challenge everything you read.

20. When an old man dies, a library is lost. (Tommy Swann)

21. Challenges can be stepping stones or stumbling–blocks. It's just a matter of how you view them.

22. If you don't stand for something, you'll fall for anything.

23. You see things the way they are and say, "Why?" I see things that never were and say, "Why not?" (George Bernard Shaw)

24. I expect to pass through life but once. If, therefore, there be any kindness I can show, or any good thing I can do to any fellow being, let me do it now, for I shall not pass this way again. (William Penn)

25. There is no future in any job. The future lies in the man who holds the job. (George Crane)

26. Train up a child in the way he should go, and when he is old, he will not depart from it. Proverbs 22:66

27. God grant me the serenity to accept the things I cannot change, courage to change the things I can, and wisdom to know the difference.

28. To be well read is to be well versed, to be illiterate is to be well cursed. R.B.

29. When you teach that children should be seen and not heard, you have just placed gasoline on the fire rather than water. R.B.

30. Either shit or get off the pot!

31. I am somebody!

32. Let there be light...

33. If you always do what you've always done, You'll always get what you've always got.

34. I penned it down and at last it came to be, for length and breadth, the bigness which you see. (John Bunyan)

20

For Your Information

FYI–1

The man who follows the crowd, will usually get no further than the crowd. The man who walks alone is likely to find himself in places no one has ever been before.

Creativity in life is not without its attendant difficulties, for peculiarity breeds contempt. And the unfortunate thing about being ahead of your time is that when people finally realize you were right, they'll say it was obvious all along.

You have two choices in life: you can dissolve into the mainstream or you can be distinct. To be distinct, you must strive to be what no one else but you can be...

By Alan Ashley–Pitt

FYI–2

All the scholars and sages of Islam have likewise given top priority to knowledge and its acquisition. Ali said to Kamil, "knowledge is better than wealth, it guards you, but you have to guard wealth, it dispenses justice while wealth seeks justice; wealth decreases with expense while knowledge increases with expenses. "Ibn Aswad said, "Nothing is more honorable than knowledge." "The kings rule over the people, while the learned rule over the kings."

FYI–3
WHAT IT TAKES TO BE NUMBER 1

YOU'VE GOT TO PAY THE PRICE.

Winning is not a sometimes thing; it's an all–the–time thing. You don't win once in a while, you don't do things right once in a while, you do them right all the time. Winning is a habit. Unfortunately, so is losing.

There is no room for second place. There is only one place in my game and this is first place. I have finished second twice in my time at Green Bay and I don't ever want to finish second again. There is a second place bowl game, but it is a game for losers played by losers. It is and always has been an American zeal to be first in anything we do, and to win, and to win, and to win.

Every time a football player goes out to ply his trade he's got to play from the group up—from the soles of his feet right up to his head. Every inch of him has to play. Some guys play with their heads. That's O.K. You've got to be smart to be No.1 in any business. But more important, you've got to play with your heart—with every fiber of your body. If you're lucky enough to find a guy with a lot of head and a lot of heart, he's never going to come off the field second.

Running a football team is no different from running any other kind of organization—an army, a political party, or a business. The principles are the same. The object is to win—to beat the other guy. Maybe that sounds cruel. I don't think it is.

It's a reality of life that men are competitive and the most competitive games draw the most competitive men. That's why they're there—to compete. They know the rules and the objectives when they get in the game. The objective is to win—fairly, squarely, decently, by the rules—but to win.

And in truth, I've never known a man worth his salt who in the long run, deep down in his heart, didn't appreciate the grind, the discipline. There is something in good men that really yearns for, need, discipline and the harsh reality of head–to–head combat.

I don't say these things because I believe in the "brute" nature of man or that men must be brutalized to be combative. I believe in God, and I believe in human decency. But I firmly believe that any man's finest hour—his greatest fulfillment to all he holds dear—is that moment when he has worked his heart out in a good cause and lies exhausted on the field of battle—victorious.

By Vince Lombardi

FYI–4

IT'S ALL IN A STATE OF MIND

If you think you are beaten you are.
If you think you dare not you don't.
If you like to win but don't think you can,
it's almost certain you won't

For many a race is lost, before a step is taken
and many a coward fails, before the fight begun.
Success begins with your will
and it's all in a state of mind.

Think big and your deeds will grow,
think small and you'll fall behind.
Think that you can and you will,
because it's all in a state of mind

Remember, life's battle doesn't always
go to the stronger or faster man,
for sooner or later the man who wins
is the one who thinks he can.

Anonymous

FYI–5

WHAT IS IT YOU WANT

Do you want money, respect,

or some sex from a person you met?

How about a loaded down car or your name on a star?

Would it matter to know that your Mom was a hoe?

Would you be a mad lad if you knew your Dad was a fag?

What is it you want?

How about a hug, a handshake, a pat on the back.

How about a job in the place of the education you lack.

Is it really your desire to climb higher and higher?

Perhaps you just want to be like the person you admire.

What is it you want?

Hey black man with the chip on his shoulder,

there's something I've learned as I got older.

Just because you're my color, don't mean you're my kind.

So the more you screw up, the more I become colorblind.

Yea I know you're black, but you can't call me brother.

You see brothers are when two people help one another.

So when you look at me, what do you see?

I bet the last thing on your mind is a family tree.

Nevertheless, I wish you the best.

Perhaps together someday we can clean up the mess.

But until that time, you're out to lunch.

That is, at least until you figure out,

WHAT IS IT YOU WANT...

By R.B.

FYI–6

DON'T QUIT

WHEN THINGS GO WRONG, as they sometimes will,
When the road you're trudging seems all uphill,
When funds are low and the debts are high,
And you want to smile, but you have to sigh,

When care is pressing you down a bit,
Rest, if you must—but don't you quit.

Life is queer with its twists and turns,
As everyone of us sometimes learns,
And many a failure turns about
When he might have won had he stuck it out;
Don't give up, though the pace seems slow—
You might succeed with another blow.

Often the goal is nearer than
It seems to a faint and faltering man,
Often the struggler has given up
When he might have captured the victor's cup.
And he learned too late, when the night slipped down
How close he was to the golden crown.
Success is failure turned inside out—

The silver tints of the clouds of doubt—
And you never can tell how close you are,
It may be near when it seems afar;
So stick to the fight when you're hardest hit—
It's when things seem worst that you mustn't quit.

FYI–7

AN EAGLE SCOUT

A different sort is an Eagle Scout
He's as good on the inside as the out.

True to his God and his nation's flag
 A boy whose loyalties never sag.

An upright boy with a heart of gold
  He can take the heat and can stand the cold.

An adventurous sort of a rough, tough lad
  He'd share with anyone, all that he had.

He's cheerful and good, and he's filled with fun
  He always helps till the work is done.

No loafer he, this young man with skill
  With his disciplined heart and mind and will.

He camps and cooks, he hikes and climbs
  He can sing a song or make verses that rhymes.

You can trust an Eagle with all you own
  You can count on him when the chips are down.

He's a splendid youth with a lifetime goal
  He's the type of boy who's in control.

A rare breed is this young Eagle Scout
  Who's as good on the inside as the out.

So honor the Eagle and model his deeds
  He'll plow rich soil and plant good seeds.

There's no better young man in this great land
  Than an Eagle Scout with a helping hand.

By Elder Vaugh J. Featherstone

FYI–8

Far better it is to dare mighty things,
to win glorious triumphs,

even though checkered by failure,
than to take rank with those poor spirits
who neither enjoy much
nor suffer much,
because they live in the gray twilight
that knows not victory
nor defeat.

By Theodore Roosevelt

FYI–9

DELINQUENT

We read in the papers and hear on the air,
Of killing and stealing and crime everywhere.
We look, sigh and say, as we notice the trend,
"This young generation... where will it all end?"
But can we be sure that it's their fault alone,
That maybe a part of it isn't our own?
Are we less guilty, who place in their way,
Too many things that lead them astray?
Too much money, too much idle time;
Too much movies of passion and crime;
Too many books not fit to be read;
Too much evil in what they hear said;
Too many children encouraged to roam;
Too many parents who don't stay at home.

Kids don't make movies; they don't write books.
They don't paint pictures of gangsters and crooks.
They don't make the laws and they don't sell the cars;
They don't make the liquor, they don't run the bars;

They don't peddle the drugs that idle the brain...
That's all done by older folks, greedy for gain.

Delinquent teenagers! Oh, how we condemn,
The sins of the nation and blame it on them.
By the laws of the blameless the Savior made known,
Who is there among us to cast the first stone?
For in so many cases—it's sad but it's true,
The title "Delinquent" fits older folks too.

FYI–10

FATHER TO SON

Son, walk with me
that I may tell you all I have seen.
Wear my shoes,
that you may learn what I have learned.
Open your heart and mind,
that I may teach you the ways of the world.
Then stand on my shoulders,
that you may see further than I
and teach me all that you see.

By R.B.

Conclusion

Figuring out life and your place in it is a journey, not an objective. One day you think you've figured everything out, and the next day you're even more confused than you were when you were searching. The truth of the matter is, you are always searching.

Why does anyone go hiking in the woods? It's because they are searching. Most hikers don't even know that they are searching, let alone what they are searching for. Generally after the hike is over, however, they are fullfilled and at peace because they have found what they were searching for—even though at the start they had know idea what they were searching for, or what they might find while hiking. They just knew that hiking was the right thing to do and in doing so, something was going to happen. So too is the nature of this book to you.

When you began reading this book, you began a journey. A journey back in time and a journey into the future. As you continued to read, my intention was to align the past and the future with your present. My intention was to assist in your navigation, to assist you in your search—your search for who <u>you</u> are.

A young man's greatest journey is the search of self. Most of the problems that exist with our youth today stems from the fact that they don't know who they are. If you knew who you were, if you were truly satisfied with who you are, then peer pressure would not even be a factor. The trends and fads would not effect you as emotionally as it does now. Your size or your color would not matter to your ego. Do you know who you are? Really, do you know who you are? Your abilities, your capabilities, your knowledge, your potential, your physical, emotional and spiritual strength, your intuition, your tenacity, your drive, your leadership, your attitude, your confidence, your personal qualities are just some of the things that make you, you. Do you know who you are, what you are made of, and all the things you can do? How powerful are you? How influential are you? Can you move mountains, can you move governments, can you move people? Who are you?

Father To Son, a guide to growing up in a difficult world has already helped many people to find themselves. Young men and young ladies have benefited greatly, not only from reading this book, but from sharing it with others who are in search of self. They have benefited from the self satisfaction feeling that they receive from helping someone else. That is the intention of this book. To help you.

It has been an awesome journey, but most important an enlightenment to manifest my thoughts into words and share them with you. Now that I am at the end, now you must begin.

May the Supreme Architect of this universe dwell and delight within you and bless you for all eternity.

ABOUT THE AUTHOR

Having gone through many difficult stages in his life, Reggie finally became an Officer in the United States Air Force, in very high profile positions. As a child, Reggie lived in the stereotypical male African American environment with a single parent mother in the Richard Allen Projects. Surviving the projects, by the time Reggie was seven, his mother saved enough money and moved Reggie and his brother Bernard to Germantown, Philadelphia, Pennsylvania.

Not having a father to guide him through his upbringing, Reggie turned to the streets for his education. Guns, gangs, drugs and crime was an everyday normality on the streets of Philadelphia. Faced with a strong desire to be successful in order to escape the streets and a need to survive, he became a young entrepreneur. He sold old newspapers and scrap metal to the junk yard, cut grass, raked leaves and shoveled snow in his neighborhood. He even worked as a door to door salesman, selling household products for Kathy Distributors.

By the time he was fifteen, he owned his own window washing business with an exclusive middle class clientele of Professors, Judges, CEO's, an FBI Agent and even the District Attorney of Philadelphia, Edward Gene Rendell, who later went on to become Mayor of Philadelphia.

When Reggie graduated from high school, he immediately left Philadelphia and worked as a camp counselor for the third time in the Pocono Mountains all summer. After returning, he went to college in New York City, where he majored in Menswear Design and Marketing, at the Fashion Institute of Technology. By the third semester, Reggie ran out of educational motivation. His fame and new found interest as a hot New York City Club DJ and desire to have fun caused his grades to slip. To prevent falling back into the street scene, Reggie quit and joined the United States Air Force as an Aircraft Weapons Specialist.

In the Air Force, Reggie found his niche and began excelling at everything he was associated with. He received countless awards, decorations and other recognition's. After he achieved all he could as a weapons specialist, he cross trained and became a recruiter. Having attended college at every tour location, he was finally able to complete his degree from F.I.T. and earn a B.S. in Education from Southern Illinois University. Unfortunately, due to new policies, Reggie was denied the opportunity to become an officer.

Reggie got out of the military, became the Director of the Philadelphia Senatorial Delegation for a few months, then relocated his family to Saudi Arabia, where he trained the Royal Saudi Air Force on the F–15 Aircraft for three years. After returning to the United States, Reggie became a Housing Manager for the very same housing authority that he had lived in. While working as a housing manager, he had also joined the Air National Guard. Shortly after joining, he was finally offered a slot as an Officer.

Once he became an officer, the Air National Guard offered him an opportunity to teach at the Academy of Military Science. He taught for two years and transitioned to Operations at the Air National Guard Headquarters, Andrews AFB, MD.

Throughout Reggie's journey, he has personally mentored over twenty youths. Worked with the Boy Scouts of America, Boys Clubs and other Youth Associations; Served as guidance counselor for misguided youth; Substitute teacher in the public school system and Vice President for Unison TV Kids. As a former Secretary of Aerospace Education and life member of the Air Force Association and NAACP, he has fought racism head on in the Blount County, Tennessee school system. In spite of the family sacrifices, the school system has undergone a major transformation of policy and staff which will benefit the future students of that school system.

Having come from humble beginnings, Reggie continues to work hard at helping others, particularly young men who do not have a father in their life. The presence of his character is felt by all who come in contact with him. He is a powerful and passionate communicator, with a determination to be himself.

Bibliography

Akbar, Na'im. <u>From Education to Miseducation</u>. Jersey City: New Mind Productions, 1982.

Al–Mizjaji, Ahmad D. <u>IT IS UP TO YOU</u>. Saudi Arabia: Sarawat Printing Press, 1987.

Bell, Janet C. <u>Famous Black Quotations</u>. Chicago: Sabayt Publications, 1986.

Hall, Manly P. <u>The Secrete Teachings of All Ages</u>. Los Angeles: The Philosophical Research Society, Inc., 1988.

Harris, Jacqueline. <u>The Tuskegee Airmen</u>. New Jersey: Dillon Press, 1996.

Kunjufu, Jawanza. <u>Lessons From History A Celebration in Blackness</u>. Elementary Edition. Chicago: African–American Images, 1987.

Kunjufu, Jawanza. <u>Lessons From History A Celebration in Blackness</u>. Jr.–SR. Edition. Chicago: African–American Images, 1987.

Lesko, Matthew. <u>Information U.S.A.</u>. New York: Penguin Books, 1986.

Louis, David. <u>2201 Fascinating Facts</u>. New York: Wings Books, 1983.

McClester, Cedric. <u>Kwanzaa: Everything You Always Wanted to Know</u>,

But Didn't Know Where to Ask. New York: Gumbs & Thomas, Publishers, Inc., 1990.

Peters, Margaret. <u>The Ebony Book of Black Achievement</u>. 2nd ed. Chicago: Johnson Publishing Company Inc., 1974

Shin, Jae C. <u>Traditional Tang Soo Do: Volume I—The Essence</u>. Philadelphia: Jae Chul Shin, 1992.

Shipley, Joseph T. <u>Dictionary of Word Origins</u>. New York: Dorset Press, 1945 MCMXLV

Tripp, Rhoda T. <u>The International Thesaurus of Quotations</u>. New York: Harper & Row, Publishers. 1970.

Vories, C. L. <u>The Hog Should It Be Used For Food?</u>. Collage Place: Color Press, 1945.

Wagman, Richard J. <u>The New Complete Medical and Health Encyclopedia</u>. Chicago: J.G. Ferguson Publishing Company, 1989.

PHOTOGRAPHS

Front Cover Head Shot—Lafayette Hills Studios, Lafayette Hills, PA

Back Cover Photo—Glen Frisco

Chapter 6—Glen Frisco

Chapter 14—Glen Frisco

Chapter 20, FYI 10—Glen Frisco

###

Printed in the United States
30700LVS00001B/328